HUNGARIAN COOKBOOK

EXPANDED EDITION

Old World Recipes for New World Cooks

Hippocrene Cookbook Library

Afghan Food & Cookery
African Cooking, Best of Regional
Albanian Cooking, Best of
Argentina Cooks!
Australia, Good Food From
Austrian Cuisine, Best of,
  Expanded Edition
Bavarian Cooking
Belgian Cookbook, A
Brazilian Cookery, The Art of
Bulgarian Cooking, Traditional
Burma, Flavors of,
Cajun Women: Recipes &
  Remembrances from South
  Louisiana Kitchens, Cooking With
Caucasus Mountains, Cuisines of the
Croatian Cooking, Best of,
  Expanded Edition
Czech Cooking, Best of,
  Expanded Edition
Danube, All Along The,
  Expanded Edition
Dutch Cooking, Art of,
  Expanded Edition
Egyptian Cooking
Eritrea, Taste of
Filipino Food, Fine
Finnish Cooking, Best of
French Caribbean Cuisine
French-English Dictionary of
  Gastronomic Terms
French Fashion, Cooking in the
  (Bilingual)
Greek Cuisine, The Best of,
  Expanded Edition
Haiti, Taste of
Havana Cookbook, Old (Bilingual)
Hungarian Cookbook
Hungarian Cooking, Art of,
  Revised Edition
Icelandic Food & Cookery
Indian Spice Kitchen
International Dictionary of
  Gastronomy
Irish-Style, Feasting Galore
Italian Cuisine, Treasury of
  (Bilingual)
Japanese Home Cooking
Korean Cuisine, Best of
Laotian Cooking, Simple
Latvia, Taste of
Lithuanian Cooking, Art of
Mayan Cooking
Mongolian Cooking, Imperial
Norway, Tastes and Tales of
Persian Cooking, Art of
Peru, Tastes of
Poland's Gourmet Cuisine
Polish Cooking, Best of,
  Expanded Edition
Polish Country Kitchen Cookbook
Polish Cuisine, Treasury of
  (Bilingual)
Polish Heritage Cookery,
  Illustrated Edition
Polish Traditions, Old
Portuguese Encounters, Cuisines of
Pyrenees, Tastes of
Quebec, Taste of
Rhine, All Along The
Romania, Taste of, Expanded Edition
Russian Cooking, Best of,
  Expanded Edition
Scandinavian Cooking, Best of
Scotland, Traditional Food From
Scottish-Irish Pub and Hearth
  Cookbook
Sephardic Israeli Cuisine
Sicilian Feasts
Slovak Cooking, Best of
Smorgasbord Cooking, Best of
South African Cookery, Traditional
South American Cookery, Art of
South Indian Cooking, Healthy
Spanish Family Cookbook,
  Revised Edition
Sri Lanka, Exotic Tastes of
Swiss Cookbook, The
Syria, Taste of
Taiwanese Cuisine, Best of
Thai Cuisine, Best of, Regional
Turkish Cooking, Art of
Turkish Cuisine, Taste of
Ukrainian Cuisine, Best of,
  Expanded Edition
Uzbek Cooking, Art of
Wales, Traditional Food From
Warsaw Cookbook, Old

HUNGARIAN COOKBOOK

EXPANDED EDITION

Old World Recipes for New World Cooks

YOLANDA NAGY FINTOR

HIPPOCRENE BOOKS, INC.
New York

Paperback edition, 2009.

Expanded Edition 2003

ISBN: 978-0-7818-1240-5

For information address:
HIPPOCRENE BOOKS, INC.
171 Madison Avenue
New York, NY 10016

Cataloging-in-Publication Data available from the Library of Congress.

Printed in the United States of America.

I dedicate this book in loving memory of:

Mark and Laura Fintor

William and Yolanda Nagy

Eugene and Verna Fintor

ACKNOWLEDGMENTS

I owe a debt of gratitude to some very special people in my life.

First, I thank my husband Ernest, with whom I share similar childhood experiences. His excellent recall of events and celebrations has helped pull memories from the deep recesses of my mind. I am grateful for his ongoing support and his willingness to make my writing life as smooth and uninterrupted as possible.

Our daughter Dawn is a talented composer and lyricist who understands the ecstasy and the agony of the creative world. She has encouraged me and lifted my spirit during the times I questioned my decision to become a writer.

Carla Henry, is a kindred spirit and a friend with whom I coauthored *Souper Skinny Soups*. Our adventure in writing a soup cookbook gave me the impetus and courage to write another cookbook. Her advice and editing assistance is greatly appreciated.

I am grateful to my top-notch writers' critique group whose constructive criticisms, tough questions, and editing skills have been of immense value. They are Bonnie Lukes, Judy Presnall, and Ruth Carlson Collier.

CONTENTS

FOREWORD

Hungarian recipes have been passed down through generations of cooks by oral tradition. This is the charm of Old World cooking: telling, listening, creating with the senses. In true Hungarian fashion, experienced cooks create meals without following written instructions. They cook by feel, taste, and sight; a pinch of this, a handful of that, a trickle of something else, until it tastes, looks, and feels right.

Under the tutelage of my Hungarian mother, questions about how much flour to combine with eggs for homemade noodles were answered with a vague "add enough flour to make the dough stick together, but not so much to make it tough. Do it enough times and you'll know."

I took her advice and soon found myself cooking with the instincts of those fine cooks before me. I worked toward refining each dish I had eaten since childhood, and once the recipe reached "perfection," recorded ingredient quantities in ink. My skill and knowledge increased when I married Ernest whose mother, Verna, was an excellent cook. She taught me even more about Hungarian cuisine.

Through the years I found I had enough recipes to share in a collected form, and *Hungarian Cookbook, Old World Recipes for New World Cooks* was born. Writing this book was not only a labor of love, it was a way to show readers that Hungarian cooking is not difficult. Recipes in this book are written so that a novice can put together a successful meal. Ingredients are not exotic; preparation instructions are detailed and easy to follow.

Another goal was to make adaptations to accommodate the lifestyle of the modern cook. In my kitchen testing of recipes, I have found that when animal fat is called for, vegetable oil is a satisfactory substitute. If making a substitution compromises the flavor, I make note of it. In many cases, I present the traditional recipe first, then, if applicable, offer a New World version so that the cook has a choice.

In keeping with today's fast-paced life, I include shortcuts wherever possible. Strudel need not be made from scratch—we now have filo dough. Store-bought egg noodles do not diminish the taste of homemade soups and stews; prune or apricot butter found in local European markets are excellent fillings for delicate pastries if you don't have the time to chop, cook, and process the fruit yourself.

My intent is to bring Old World cooking into today's kitchens where the convenience of modern products and sophisticated equipment make this culinary art easy, enjoyable, and satisfying.

A visiting Englishman asked me the secret of the Hungarian cuisine. I told him: "It is sweet onions, noble paprika, unmatched bacon, the best sour cream and a thousand years experience."

— Anonymous Restaurateur

INTRODUCTION

A Glimpse into Hungary's Culinary History

Hungary's beginnings have been traced to an ancient homeland near the Ural mountains on the border of Europe and Asia. From these mountains, nomadic tribes called Magyars traveled southwest. In A.D. 896 they settled in what is now Hungary.

The Magyars retained their ancient method of cooking outdoors, using heavy kettles in which to cook their meat. They sat around these large pots dipping their bread into the mixture of meat and vegetables that came to be known as goulash (*gulyás*), Hungary's unofficial national dish.

Hungary became a kingdom in A.D. 1001 under the reign of St. Stephen. The following 300 years were turbulent. The Crusades passed through Hungary with violent force, and Tatar invasions almost destroyed the country. But in the wake of this devastation came new customs, new habits, and new recipes.

Hungarian cuisine entered a period of development and refinement during the reign of King Matthias (1458–1490). His marriage to Beatrice, daughter of an Italian king brought many changes into Matthias's kitchen.

Beatrice introduced cheeses, pastries, chestnuts, anise, onion, garlic, dill, capers, and other unfamiliar delicacies. She also initiated the use of fine dinnerware. Beatrice was responsible for incorporating music with meals and, still today, we hear the romantic strains of the violinist who entertains us in fine Hungarian restaurants.

In 1526, the Turkish invasion led to the fragmentation of the country, and for the next 150 years Hungary was a nation of upheaval. Three sections emerged as a result of the split: (1) Transylvania, an independent principality; (2) Hapsburg-ruled western and northern areas; and (3) the central region, which was under Turkish occupation. This division, however painful, was instrumental in laying the foundation for modern Hungarian cuisine. These outside influences brought new cooking methods, foods and spices.

The Turks introduced Hungarians to paprika, a spice embraced for its color and flavor, and now a favorite of Hungarian cooks. Other Turkish contributions were coffee, tomatoes, corn, squash, eggplant, noodles with cottage cheese, stuffed peppers, and strudel. Stuffed cabbage already was an established meal among the ancient Magyars.

French cuisine reached Hungarian cooks through the Hapsburg influence. The blending of French and Hungarian cooking methods tempered the strongly spiced base of Hungarian cooking styles.

Transylvania, now part of Rumania, has been inhabited by Rumanians, Hungarians, and Germans. Food historians claim that, because of its historical and geographical advantages, Transylvania has developed the most interesting culinary practices in the Hungarian kitchen.

We can see how the intermingling of cultures throughout Hungary's history has resulted in a unique and outstanding cuisine that found its way to the New World. Hungarians who arrived in America in the late nineteenth and early twentieth centuries brought with them time-tested recipes committed to memory rather than to paper. Settling near each other, Hungarians perpetuated their traditions through social functions of the church, or through fraternal and cultural clubs.

First- and second-generation children learned to dance the twirling *csárdás* at these functions that began with the singing of the Hungarian national anthem. This solemn, mournful song was a sharp contrast to the festivities that followed: dancing to a live band of violins accompanied by the dulcimer-like instrument, the cimbalom; eating traditional foods like goulash, stuffed cabbage, and melt-in-your-mouth homemade pastries.

This is my heritage. I am the product of a culture that loves lively music, feverish dancing, and good food. The recipes in this book reflect this history and come directly from Hungarian kitchens via grandparents, aunts, in-laws, cousins, and friends. *Jó étvágyot kivánok* (I wish you a good appetite).

CHARACTERISTICS OF THE HUNGARIAN LANGUAGE

- The Hungarian language is phonetic in that all letters are pronounced.
- There are no mute vowels; even final vowels are spoken.
- The stress always falls on the first syllable.
- When Hungarians refer to or address one another, the surname is said first.
- Accent marks over vowels indicate long vowel sounds, and, as in Spanish or Italian, the tongue always rolls the *r*.
- There is no distinction of gender in pronouns.
- Some nouns denote male or female (ex. *Testvér* means brother or sister).

Pronunciation of Vowels:

a = uh
á = ah
e = eh
é = ay (long a)
i = short i
í = ee (as in sleep)
ó = oh
ú = oo (as in coo)
ö = u (as in fur)

Pronunciation of these Consonants is Unique to Hungarian Speech:

s = sh (*kis* is pronounced kish); means "little"

sz = s (*szép* is pronounced sayp); means "pretty"

cs = ch (*csárdás* is pronounced chahrdahsh); means "two-step folk dance"

zs = *zseb* (zs has same sound as the s in measure or zs in Zsa-Zsa); means "pocket"

j = y (*haj* is pronounced huy, short u sound); means "hair"

ny = ni (*nyár* is pronounced niahr, as in onion); means "summer"

gy = dy (Magyar is pronounced Mudyahr, not Mag-yar)

w = v

ly = y (*gyulyás* is pronounced gooyahsh); means "goulash"

BASIC GUIDELINES

Unless otherwise indicated:

(1) The sugar used in recipes is granulated.

(2) The flour used is white, all-purpose.

(3) The butter used is salted.

(4) Oven or liquid temperatures are in Fahrenheit degrees.

(5) Ingredients are at room temperature.

(6) All measures are standard and should be level.

(7) Vinegar is distilled white.

(8) Shortening is hydrogenated fat made from vegetable oils.

STAPLES

Your food pantry and refrigerator probably contain most of the ingredients you will need:

Bacon
Thick-sliced bacon is best for most recipes. Buy bacon slabs for Bacon Cookout (page 21).

Bouillon cubes
These cubes come in beef, chicken, fish, and vegetable flavors and may be used in place of fresh broth. Follow the package directions for dilution.

Dill
Fresh or dried may be used, but be mindful that dried herbs are three times stronger than the fresh. If substituting dry dill for fresh, adjust the amounts accordingly. You want this herb to enhance, not to overwhelm.

Paprika
Fiery red, but mildly sweet, paprika adds color and flavor to meat, noodles, stews, and vegetables. Buy paprika imported from Szeged, Hungary for true flavor. Most grocery stores carry it and it is not expensive.

Parsley
The flat-leafed Italian parsley (not to be confused with cilantro) is best for soups, stews, dumplings, and garnishes. If you can find the leaves still attached to the root, use the whole plant for added flavor when making soup.

Poppy seed
This is not a common ingredient, but is used in many dessert recipes. When a recipe calls for ground poppy seeds, use a blender

or food processor to grind whole seeds. One-half pound of whole poppy seeds makes about 2½ cups when ground. Specialty stores carry this.

Potatoes

White rose or red rose refers to thin-skinned white or red potatoes that can be cooked and eaten with the skin on, as opposed to Idaho or russet potatoes that have thicker skins.

Rice

My preference is long-grained, converted rice as it does not lump together when cooked. 1 cup of raw rice yields 3 cups cooked rice.

Saffron

Threads of saffron give soup and rice dishes a deep golden hue. Unlike paprika, saffron diffuses color as it is sprinkled over warm food. At around $83.00 an ounce, these precious reddish-orange threads are sold in grams and kept under lock and key at grocery stores. The price reflects the intensive labor required to collect stigmas from each flower. It takes between 85,000 and 250,000 stigmas to produce one pound of saffron, and they must be collected by hand.

Sour cream

Use a name brand; some of the off-brands may be too watery. Low-fat sour cream may be substituted, if desired.

Walnuts

Use fresh walnuts. Your food processor will make short work of chopping or grinding nuts.

Yeast

Either dry yeast in envelopes or yeast cakes may be used. Be sure to check the expiration date on the package. Old yeast will inhibit your dough from rising. (See tip #6 on page 10).

TIPS

1. To shorten food preparation time, use a blender or food processor.

   (a) Use a blender or the chopping blade of a food processor to chop or grind nut meats. Fruit and vegetables such as apples, carrots, onions, and green peppers must be cut into 1-inch pieces and processed ½ cup at a time in a blender; 1 cup at a time in a food processor.

   (b) Sugar can be made finer (for quick dissolving) by processing on high speed ½ cup at a time.

   (c) To make bread crumbs, tear one slice of fresh bread to pieces, or break up a slice of dry bread, into a blender. Press the medium speed button and blend for 5 seconds at a time. Use the chopping blade if using a food processor. Process until fine crumbs form.

2. If you only need half an onion, save the root half. It will last longer.

3. Soak chicken in salted water or buttermilk for extra tenderness.

4. If you forgot to buy the buttermilk, add 1 tablespoon vinegar to 1 cup milk and use as a substitute.

5. Soak leafy vegetables in cold, salted water to remove small, hard-to-see insects.

•

6. When dissolving yeast in warm liquid, use a meat/yeast thermometer. The temperature of milk, water, or melted butter should be 105 to 115 degrees to assure successful rising of dough.

7. To defrost a frozen turkey, use this rule of thumb: for every 5 pounds of turkey, allow 24 hours of thawing time in the refrigerator. For example, a 15-pound turkey will take 3 days to defrost.

8. When cooking cauliflower, add lemon juice to keep it snowy white.

9. Use powdered sugar instead of flour when rolling and cutting cookies. They will be lighter and more flavorful.

10. A splash of 1 to 2 tablespoons of vinegar to the pot gives legume soups an added punch of flavor.

GLOSSARY

Braise – to brown small pieces of meat, poultry, or fish before simmering in a small amount of liquid

Brining – soaking meat or chicken in salt water to make it tender and juicy

Broth – liquid made with fish, meat, poultry, or vegetables for soup

Cimbalom – large version of a dulcimer; played in Hungarian bands

Crescent shape – refers to cookies with a nut or fruit filling, that are rolled and bent into a crescent shape before baking

Csárdás – a fast two-step folk dance

Dice – to chop food into small pieces

Dredge – to cover with flour before browning

Dressing – stuffing for meat and poultry; usually made of bread, eggs, herbs, and vegetables, but can be made of fruit or nuts

Dry cottage cheese – also called farmer's cheese; it is usually sweetened and used in dessert recipes

Dutch oven – a large, high-sided, heavy-bottomed skillet, with a cover

Egg barley – small pieces of noodles made of eggs and flour; not to be confused with pearl barley, a natural grain

Egg wash – a mixture of egg yolk and water brushed on baked goods to make them shiny

Filo or phyllo dough – tissue-thin sheets of dough which are layered, spread with a filling, and rolled; available in frozen section of grocery stores

Folding – a gentle blending of whipped egg whites into a thick batter; always done by hand rather than with a mixer

Giblets – the gizzard, heart, and liver of poultry

Knead – to push dough against pastry board using the heel of both hands

Mince – to chop very fine, almost to a grated texture

Pastry blender – a kitchen tool made of a row of blades to cut shortening into flour

Pastry board – an oversized bread board, used to roll out dough

Peppercorns – kernels of whole pepper used for cooking or for grinding

Roux – a mixture of flour browned in fat and used to thicken gravy and soup

Sauté – to cook meat, chicken, fish, or vegetables on low heat, uncovered

Score – to cut across a fatty layer of meat or skin (as in a ham)

Simmer–to bring liquids to a gentle boil; the best temperature for cooking soups and stews

Sliver – to cut food into thin slices, lengthwise, as with garlic or almonds

Truss – to close the opening of poultry cavity with pins and string, or to roll and tie a flat piece of meat into a roast

Tureen – a deep serving dish for soup

Whisk – a wire utensil used for whipping out lumps when mixing dry ingredients and liquids

Zest – grated rind of a lemon or an orange

Old Hungarian saying:
"We may be poor, but our stomachs
are always full."

HUMBLE BEGINNINGS

In the early 1900s, Grandma and Grandpa Nagy emigrated from Hungary to America where the young couple settled in the urban hills of Pittsburgh, Pennsylvania. My father William, his two sisters, and a brother were born within the next nine years. Grandpa provided for his growing family by working for the Pennsylvania Railroad Company.

When my father married Yolanda, a young Hungarian émigré, he brought her into a two-story frame house he shared with his parents and siblings, which, by then, included a married sister. I was born the following year. My sister Elsie was born two years later, and sister Dolly, two years after Elsie. (Baby Brother Bill was born after his three sisters were in their teens). The birth of my cousins, Lillian and Barbara, rounded out this extended household of three generations.

Grandpa was the patriarch. His word was the highest authority, but Grandma ruled the kitchen. My father, as the oldest son, was next in the chain of command, with his youngest sibling at the bottom. As undemocratic as this seems today, the system worked because of the respect the younger age group had for the one before it. Economic necessity for this arrangement outweighed the friction that must have erupted occasionally. Unaware of adult problems, I thought it was great fun living with Grandma and Grandpa, Uncle Andy, Aunt Ethel, her husband, Uncle Steve, my cousins, and my sisters. Besides, this lifestyle was common to everyone we knew, for this was the decade of the Great Depression.

Author's first home with grandparents in Pittsburgh, PA.

Today, when I see historical news footage depicting the bread lines of the 1930s, I try to recall memories of a stomach aching from hunger and I have none. Money was scarce but there was always food on the table, however humble.

Many of our suppers consisted of bread soaked in sweetened warm milk. This soggy food filled our bellies and kept us satisfied until the next simple meal. I learned much later that this was a traditional recipe served often in the Hungarian village where my grandparents had lived.

MILK SOUP
Tejleves

4 cups whole milk
1 cup water
2 tablespoons sugar
¼ teaspoon salt
2 cups white bread, torn into chunks

Heat milk, water, sugar, and salt until hot, but not boiling. Pour into soup bowls and add bread.

SERVES 4

In the summer, vegetables from a large garden behind the house sustained us. Whatever was not eaten fresh was canned for winter enjoyment. For my sisters, my cousins, and me, the great thrill was reaching into bushel baskets of freshly picked vegetables and pulling out ripe tomatoes that spurted juice all over us when we bit into them. At harvest time, sugar-sweet peas, tender green beans, and crunchy carrots were our snacks. Grandma and Grandpa also grew cabbage, lettuce, green onions, dill, radishes, green peppers, corn, cucumbers, kohlrabi, and parsley with roots a foot long. This garden was our mainstay of fresh ingredients for nourishing meals, many of which I continue to cook today.

In Praise of a Sow

Your grace, your most gracious Majesty!
Thus I courted the four-hundred-pound sow,
when grunting she approached me—
Love's passion's fine work raises us to
human dignity; but a handsome porker
can also be praised by the poet's art!
— Jozseg Berda, Hungarian poet

PIG IN THE BASEMENT

When the nation's economy improved, the aroma of smoked meat filled the air. My father and two uncles drove the old family Dodge to a farm and brought back a slaughtered pig to butcher. A large wooden table in the basement served as the butcher block. I stayed around only long enough to watch the men sharpen their knives, then retreated to the backyard to play with my sisters and cousins. I did not return until I smelled portions of pig skin frying in large pans on the basement stove Grandma used to boil bleach water on washdays. Skillets sizzled with the rendered fat that would later be used in family recipes.

For us children, this was the best part of the proceedings. Our first stop was the kitchen where we grabbed slices of freshly baked bread. We then ran down to the basement and headed for the stove. We scooped out spoonfuls of the crispy cracklings (*tepertö)* onto our bread and hurried back upstairs leaving the adults to their work.

The women continued rendering fat while the men ground part of the meat in a meat grinder. They cut other parts into ham hocks, pork chops, bacon, ribs, and steaks. Most of the ground meat was made into spicy garlic-laden sausages (*kolbász*), or blood and liver sausages (*húrka*). We children sometimes helped tie off the casings after the stuffer filled them with the meat mixture.

All the cuts of meat were put into large tubs and carried to the backyard smokehouse for curing. I remember sniffing the aromatic smoke as it wafted though the air and I imagined I could taste the meals that were to come from that little building.

MEMORIES OF HUNGARIAN EASTERS

As Protestants, my family's day of abstinence from meat was Good Friday. But many of my Catholic friends ate meatless meals throughout the forty days of Lent. A variety of vegetable soups and noodle casseroles became staples during Lent. It is no wonder that in the Hungarian language, Easter is called *Husvét*. Loosely translated, it means "now the meat."

Easter Sunday marked our family's first church outing for new spring outfits and white shoes. When we returned from services, however, the whole family removed their Sunday clothes and changed into weekday attire (unless company was expected).

In the 1940s and 1950s men, women, and even children wore hats to church and to other important occasions, but under no circumstances did anyone intentionally place a hat on the bed. According to folk legend, such carelessness would almost certainly lead to the imminent death of a loved one. This superstition became so ingrained that, to this day, I cannot put a hat on my bed, or any other bed.

Sprinkling Day was celebrated the Monday after Easter. Preteen boys and girls acted out this transplanted European custom with squeals and giggles under the watchful eyes of the girls' parents.

The ritual began with a knock on the door. When Mother or Father answered, there stood a boy (usually two boys showed up, each bolstering the other with courage) that my sisters and I knew from school or church.

They nervously recited a poem in Hungarian. Translated the poem said:

> "As I passed by your house the other day, I looked upon your garden. And to my dismay I noticed your beautiful flowers wilting. May I have your permission to sprinkle them?"

What they were asking to do was to sprinkle us with perfume. Our parents always granted permission for they had grown up with this practice and even encouraged it. Of course, my sisters and I had heard the knock on the door and were already on the run by the time the boys gave chase. If we didn't like the boys, we tried very hard not to get caught. But, if we liked them we didn't run very fast. Getting doused with cheap toilet water was fun only if we liked the chasers. The enthusiastic visitors then received their prizes from our mother or father. The reward could be colored hard-boiled eggs or candy, but usually it was a few cents in change. The enterprising young men then went on to the next house and the next and on and on. My husband tells me that he made a fair amount of change on Easter Mondays those many years ago.

These were typical Easter weekend menus in many Hungarian households:

Good Friday

Kohlrabi Soup (page 66)
Mushroom Paprika (page 143)
Baked Noodles (page 84)

Easter Sunday

Glazed Ham with Horseradish Relish (page 126, 38)
Hard-boiled eggs
Hungarian Sausage, fresh and smoked (page 115)
Sour Cream Potato Salad (page 49)
Sweet and Sour Cabbage (page 141)
Walnut Roll (page 178)

BACON COOKOUT
Szalonna Sutés

Summer meant the backyard filled with the aroma of smoke-cured bacon squares, skewered on a stick and frying over an open fire. Thick slices of rye bread, covered with diced red radishes, chopped green pepper, and chunks of white onions, waited to catch the dripping bacon grease.

Unless you butcher your own pig, you will need to purchase slabs of bacon (unsliced). These are sold at specialty markets sold in approximately 4 × 8-inch rectangles. Each slab serves two people. Prepare bacon for the barbecue in this manner:

1. Score the bacon down *to*, but not *through* the rind in tic-tac-toe fashion; cut about a 2 × 4-inch section from the slab for each person.
2. Skewer each section on its own long fork or stick and hold over the fire until bacon sizzles and drips grease.
3. Pull bacon away from the flame and hold over the rye bread and vegetables, allowing the drippings to soak into the bread. Return bacon to cook over the flame
4. Continue the cook-and-drip procedure until your slice of bread is saturated with as much of the bacon drippings as you desire.
5. When the bacon becomes crispy, cut it away from the rind; dice the bacon and spread over bread and vegetables.

Chewing on the rind was (and still is) as pleasurable as eating the bacon flavored bread. My family continues the tradition of this Hungarian-style barbecue, but we limit our indulgence to about once a year.

Summer also meant savoring the taste of the sun in freshly picked corn-on-the-cob. When Detroit heat boiled our blood, we escaped by piling into the old Dodge and driving to the farm where our friends lived. In those days, families didn't have to wait for an invitation to visit. A phone call telling friends to expect company was a common practice. Even unexpected guests were welcomed with graciousness and refreshments.

When we arrived, we smelled corn cooking in a huge pot on an outdoor stove. A picnic table was set with large tin plates, napkins, and saltshakers—nothing else! The corn was so sweet it didn't need butter. To me, this was the ultimate feast. I ate cob after cob, stopping only when I could hold no more and felt ready to burst. However, after a few games of hide-and-seek and climbing trees in the apple orchards, I was ready for more corn.

It was from this warm family that my mother learned the simplicity of cooking corn and retaining its freshness:

BOILED CORN-ON-THE-COB

6 to 8 quarts water
6 to 8 ears corn

Bring water to a boil in a large pot. Remove husks and corn silk from each ear. Place the corn into boiling water; cover. When water returns to a full boil, turn off the heat immediately. Leave covered and corn will finish cooking in its own steam, about 10 minutes.

MICROWAVED CORN-ON-THE-COB

Remove corn silk, but leave most of the husk on ears of corn. Place up to 4 ears in a microwave dish, cover, and microwave on high allowing 3 minutes per ear.

Summer Menus

Bacon Cookout (page 21)
Corn-on-the-Cob (page 22, 23)
Coleslaw (page 46)

Hot Dog Stew (page 135)
Potato Salad (page 49)

Chilled Creamed Green Bean Soup (page 64)
Vegetables and Rice (page 145)

"Of the four main ingredients—wine, wheat, peace and a beautiful woman, wine is mentioned first."

— Old Hungarian Expression

GRAPE FESTIVAL
Szüreti Bál

As indelible as my early Hungarian family memories are, ethnic awareness did not fully ripen until Dad moved us to Detroit, Michigan, in search of better job opportunities. Not surprisingly, we settled in an area where many Hungarians lived, sharing a community with families of other nationalities, mostly Armenian, Black, Gypsy, Italian, Jewish, and Polish.

This multiethnic flavor was reflected in the faces of children at my neighborhood school. And it was the school system that opened the gates of ethnic understanding for me through its promotion of international programs. At special assemblies, families brought foods that were representative of their culture. Children from each nationality performed folk dances unique to their family background. We even learned popular phrases of one another's language.

Music and dance permeate almost every Hungarian festivity. And, thanks to fraternal organizations, churches, and cultural clubs, Old World customs are perpetuated. A popular event that is still celebrated in October is the Grape Festival *(Szureti Bál)*. Grape leaves decorate the halls, women and girls don native Hungarian dresses, and a string ensemble fills the room with stirring strains of folk music. This festive affair dates back to the sixteenth century when the harvesting of grapes was cause for celebration in Hungarian towns where vineyards often covered several acres of land.

Hungarians coming to America preserved the grape festival celebration by bringing along the colorful holiday costumes from the Old World. Mothers sewed new costumes for their American-born children when they reached the age of participation. A single dress had a skirt with fifty to one hundred pleats that were ironed by hand into sharp points. The bodice was made of a vest of red velvet decorated with sequins, beads, and gold braid. White, puffy sleeves were sewn into the vest; red and green satin ribbons decorated a starched, white apron worn over the skirt. Festive attire for the men and boys was simpler: black trousers and vests; white shirts with full billowing sleeves and black boots for those who could afford them.

Properly costumed, these first- and second-generation Hungarian Americans learned a special dance that they performed in a large hall. The performers entered the hall in couples singing the grape harvesting song, *Meg Éret*, a song that speaks of the ripening of black grapes. When the group of eight to ten couples completes the routine, everyone in the hall grabs a partner and dances the *csárdás*, a fast two-step that ends with partners twirling in dizzying circles until the music stops.

In the past, fraternal club or church members cooked the superb food that was served. And still today, in close-knit Hungarian communities throughout America, dedicated men and women donate their time to cook and serve for special events. But in most metropolitan areas, where the Hungarian population is spread far and wide, the work is contracted to caterers who specialize in ethnic cooking. It is not quite the same, although now, as then, there is usually a choice of two or three entrees. The following menu is typical of food served at this lively fall festival:

Goulash (page 117, 118)
Stuffed Cabbage (page 110)
Hungarian Sausage (page 115)
Cucumber Salad (page 47, 48)
Strudel (page 180)

Hungarian dancers.

"Food is a wonderful way of celebrating a special time as well as a way of just bringing people together."

— Actress Phylicia Rashad, host
For Pillsbury's 50th Anniversary
Million Dollar Bake-off

WEDDINGS

As soon as the wedding invitations were mailed, Mother received phone calls from relatives and friends. The calls were not so much of a congratulatory nature as they were offerings of food and pastries for the reception—a custom brought to the New World by immigrants and practiced by first- and second-generation Hungarian-Americans well into the twentieth century.

Aunt Ethel wanted to bring *kalács* (walnut rolls); Aunt Katherine, *kifli* (fruit or nut-filled crescent cookies); Aunt Emma, her famous *dobos torta* (7-layer glazed torte). Mrs. Varga promised her flaky *almás rétes* (apple strudel), while Mrs. Horvath could be counted on for a big pot of *töltött káposzta* (stuffed cabbage).

A week before the wedding, pounds of butter, flour, sour cream, and walnuts were baked into dozens of cookies and pastries by Mother and her "kitchen brigade," each in her own home. A day or two before the wedding, Mother made several quarts of potato salad, chilled the homemade dill pickles, and baked not only a ham, but several pounds of *kolbász* (Hungarian sausages) as well. She ordered loaves of delicatessen rye bread from the same bakery that baked the wedding cake, a chore she preferred to turn over to professionals.

But, using the services of a caterer never entered the picture. This tradition of family and friends bringing food was a reciprocal activity. Those that received always had an opportunity to return the favor at the next wedding. This interweaving of giving and receiving kept alive the traditions and the closeness of the community.

The groom's family was responsible for buying liquid refreshments and for hiring musicians. The band usually included two violinists, a pianist, and a bassist. When available, a musician who played the cimbalom joined the band. The cimbalom, a large version of a dulcimer, is played with two soft-tipped mallets striking a string of keys. The sound adds the romantic mellowness of a harp. Folk-dance music we had all known since childhood filled the reception hall and everybody danced.

Long after the bride and groom departed, the old-timers, fortified with beer or wine, gathered around the piano to sing the songs they had learned in Hungary so many years ago.

Cimbalom.

Musician playing cimbalom.

BAPTISMS

"First comes love, then comes marriage,
Then comes Yolanda with a baby carriage."

In my generation, a young woman's destiny mirrored this childhood ditty. Our first child was born a year after my marriage to Ernest. Mark was baptized at five months of age, once more bringing together family members and close friends. The food served after the church ceremony was again supplied in potluck style, but not as elaborate as the wedding reception. The cake, however, had to be white for purity, and it had to be baked or supplied by the godparents.

Many old wives' tales surfaced at this gathering. Older relatives solemnly warned us never to allow our baby to view his image in a mirror until after he reached a year old because this could cause mental retardation. A more positive admonition was that if you shave off a baby's first growth of hair before age one, he will always have a thick head of hair. We were also told we must put shoes on the baby after he began to walk or he would develop flat feet. And never cut a baby's nails with scissors—the mother, and only the mother, must shorten them by biting the nails with her teeth. Why? Because if anyone but his mother bites the baby's nails, ill health will befall him! The advice that disturbed us the most was: don't pick up a crying baby once he's been fed and diapered—you'll spoil him. No wonder so many of us turned to Dr. Spock for guidance!

"Crumbs spilled on the table during Christmas dinner can be planted to grow marinka, *a sweet smelling flower."*
— Hungarian folklore

CHRISTMAS AND NEW YEAR
Goose and Pigs' Feet

Christmas goose, roasted until the skin got crispy, was the special meal we enjoyed Christmas Day. Mother served it with stuffing, giblet gravy, baked sweet potatoes, and creamed green beans. Since goose has no white meat, there was no need to fight over drumsticks and thighs, only over who got the wishbone.

The true meaning of Christmas was never lost during those early years. Christmas Eve church services always included the children and we faithfully attended. Our parents proudly watched as my sisters and I sang Christmas carols in both English and Hungarian with the Sunday school choir. In later years we learned to sing "Oh Come All Ye Faithful" and "Ave Maria" in Latin and thought of ourselves as terribly worldly and multilingual.

We didn't have an abundance of gifts. Many a Christmas morning, my sisters and I would find only one gift from Santa for the three of us to share. However, other surprises under the tree represented hours of secretly gluing, pasting, sewing, crocheting, or knitting homemade gifts for one another. My youngest sibling Bill, sisters Elsie and Dolly, and I continue this tradition of making, rather than purchasing gifts for one another. These gifts have accumulated over the years and each one occupies a special place in our homes and hearts.

Christmas Day Menu

Roasted Goose with Bread Stuffing (page 100, 106)
Giblet Gravy (page 102)

Creamed Peas (page 150)
Baked Yams
Cucumber Salad (page 47, 48)
Crescent Cookies (page 171–175)
Walnut Roll (page 178–179)

On New Year's Eve morning, the aroma of pigs' feet, onion, and garlic simmering in a large pot filled the kitchen. *Kocsonya* had to be made the day before eating because it took 24 hours for the broth to jell in the refrigerator (see page 123 for recipe). Mother had large soup bowls and each held one large, or two small feet. She poured the broth over the cooked feet and liberally sprinkled paprika into each bowl. The next day we scraped off the solid fat from the surface of the dishes and enjoyed cold pig's feet and jelled broth with thick slices of rye bread.

While my mother-in-law followed the tradition of making pigs' feet for New Year, she was also a great believer in serving black-eyed peas. She felt this would bring her family good luck during the coming year. Ernest remembers that when good things happened, no one took notice. But, when something unfortunate befell any of the family, she would say, "See, you didn't have enough of those lucky peas New Year's Day."

New Year's Day Menu

Jellied Pigs' Feet (page 123)
Baked Ham (page 126)
Hungarian Sausage (page 115)
Potato Salad (page 48, 50)
Sweet and Sour Cabbage (page 141)
Rye bread

Appetizers, Relishes, and Sauces

CHICKEN LIVER PATÉ
Csirkemáj Pástétom

Even those who do not like chicken liver will find this paté quite tasty. Serve this appetizer with crackers or crisp dry toast.

1 pound chicken livers, rinsed and drained (goose liver may be substituted)
1 cup chopped onion
4 tablespoons butter
3 hard-boiled eggs, chopped
1 teaspoon salt
½ teaspoon dry mustard
1 teaspoon paprika
¼ teaspoon freshly ground pepper

Sauté chicken livers and onion in butter for 10 minutes. Turn liver pieces over, cover and cook 10 minutes longer, or until livers are no longer pink in the center.

Cool; cut livers into quarters. Place one egg and one-third of the liver mixture with drippings into a blender container or food processor. Cover and pulse on high speed for 10 seconds. Remove liver/egg combination from the blender to a bowl. Repeat this procedure two more times. When blending is complete, add salt, dry mustard, paprika, and pepper. Chill in refrigerator 4 hours.

MAKES 2 TO 2½ CUPS

NEW WORLD CHICKEN LIVER SPREAD

1 pound chicken livers
1 cup chopped onion
2 tablespoons vegetable oil
½ teaspoon salt
¼ teaspoon pepper
1 teaspoon paprika

Proceed cooking and processing livers and onion as above.

MAKES 1½ CUPS

CUCUMBER DILL DIP
Uborka Kapor Előéttelt

1 package (8 ounces) cream cheese, room temperature
½ cup sour cream
½ cup shredded, unpeeled cucumber, well drained
½ teaspoon Worcestershire sauce
¼ teaspoon dry dill or 2 teaspoons finely chopped fresh dill
1 clove garlic, minced

Combine cream cheese and sour cream. Add cucumber, Worcestershire sauce, dill, and garlic. Blend well and chill 1 hour. Serve with raw vegetables or potato chips.

MAKES 1½ CUPS

NEW WORLD CUCUMBER DILL DIP

8 ounces plain yogurt
¼ cup shredded, unpeeled cucumber, well drained
¼ teaspoon Worcestershire sauce
¼ teaspoon dry dill or 2 teaspoons finely chopped fresh dill
¼ teaspoon garlic salt

Combine yogurt, cucumber, Worcestershire sauce, dill, and garlic salt; mix well. Chill 1 hour before serving with vegetables or chips.

MAKES 1 CUP

Sour Cream-Parsley Dip.

SOUR CREAM-PARSLEY DIP
Petrezselymes Tejfel-Előétel

1 cup sour cream
2 tablespoons chopped fresh parsley
2 tablespoons chopped fresh chives
1 teaspoon lemon juice
Dash garlic salt
3 to 4 drops hot pepper sauce

Thoroughly blend all ingredients and chill.

MAKES 1 CUP

HORSERADISH RELISH
Torma Mártás

My father always went out to the back porch to grate this highly potent vegetable, fresh from the garden. He put a bowl between his knees, a handkerchief around his nose and, using a handheld grater, went to work. Grating this thick root burned the eyes, but today we have the food processor to speed up the job and spare us the tears.

This relish pairs well with ham, beef, chicken, or fish. Mix into seafood cocktail sauce for added zip.

1 horseradish root, peeled and diced
1 to 2 teaspoons cider vinegar
½ teaspoon salt
1 teaspoon sugar

Place the root in a food processor. Process until finely chopped. Pour in cider vinegar until the mixture is of spreading consistency. Add salt and sugar. Adjust seasonings to taste.

Placed in a covered container, this keeps several months in the refrigerator.

MAKES 1 CUP

GARLICKY DILL PICKLES
Fokhagymás Uborka Kaporral

Pickles "sun-cooked" in brine are crunchy and easy to make. The hard part is waiting out the two or three days it takes for the pickles to "cure."

1 quart jar
6 to 8 large pickling cucumbers
1 quart water
1½ tablespoons coarse salt
2 dill stems and seed heads
3 cloves garlic
1 slice Jewish rye bread

Thoroughly wash and dry the jar. Wash the pickles and slice into fourths lengthwise, but not all the way through. This allows the brine to flow through the pickles.

Boil the water with the salt. Set one dill stem into the bottom of the jar. Cut in half or into fourths if necessary. Place pickles over the dill, standing them on end. Add garlic and place a dill stem over the pickles. Pour boiling water into the jar, covering the pickles completely.

Cool to lukewarm: place bread on top of the pickles and a plate over the bread (to keep the birds out).

Set the bottle where the sun will shine on it for several hours a day. After two days the pickles will lose their bright green look. Check for crispness. If pickles are not crisp enough, leave the jar out another day.

When the pickles have reached the correct crispness, refrigerate.

MAKES 1 QUART

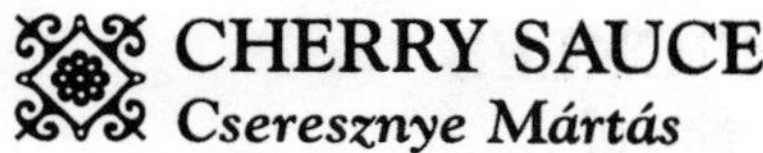

CHERRY SAUCE
Cseresznye Mártás

Hungarians sometimes like to eat chicken parts separately from the soup in which they cooked. The chicken is then served as a second course with cherry sauce on the side. Cherry sauce over chicken or potatoes is a unique palate pleaser.

2 tablespoons flour
2 tablespoons butter
1 can (15 ounces) pitted cherries, including juice
1 tablespoon lemon juice
1 teaspoon sugar
Pinch of salt
½ cup light cream
2 tablespoons sour cream

In a 2-quart saucepan, lightly brown flour in butter. Add cherries with juice, lemon juice, sugar, and salt. Bring to a slow boil, until thickened. Combine cream and sour cream, add to sauce, and cook on low heat 5 minutes longer. This sauce can be served warm, cold, or room at temperature.

MAKES 2½ CUPS

NEW WORLD CHERRY SAUCE

1 can (15 ounces) pitted cherries, including juice
1 tablespoon lemon juice
1 teaspoon sugar
Pinch of salt
2 tablespoons cornstarch
½ cup milk

Combine cherries, lemon juice, sugar, and salt. Bring to a gentle boil. In a small bowl, mix cornstarch into milk. Add to cherry mixture and simmer 5 minutes until sauce is thickened.

MAKES 2½ CUPS

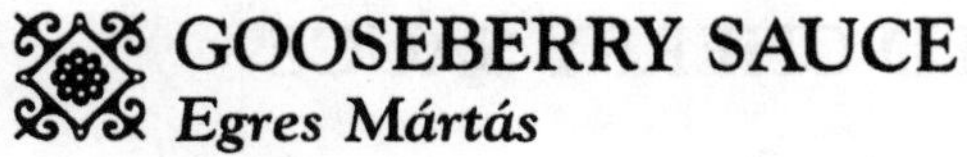

GOOSEBERRY SAUCE
Egres Mártás

This sauce is a creamy, but light accompaniment to any meat.

8 ounces gooseberries, washed, stems removed
¼ cup sugar
2 thin slices lemon
2 cups water
¼ cup white wine
¼ cup sour cream
1 tablespoon all-purpose flour

Combine gooseberries with sugar, lemon slices, water, and wine. Cover and simmer 15 to 20 minutes.

In a small bowl, mix the sour cream and flour. To this mixture slowly add ½ cup of the hot gooseberry broth while whipping into a smooth paste. Use a wooden spoon or a whisk to whip.

Pour the paste into the cooked fruit; mix well. Continue to cook on low heat while stirring for about 5 minutes, or until the taste of flour is gone. Turn off the heat and allow the sauce to sit a few minutes before serving.

MAKES 2½ TO 3 CUPS

TOMATO SAUCE
Paradicsom Mártás

2 tablespoons butter
1½ cups chopped onion
2 tablespoons flour
4 fresh tomatoes, diced, or 1 can (15 ounces) diced tomatoes
¼ teaspoon sugar

Melt butter; sauté onions in butter until browned. Add flour to onions; stir while flour browns. Mix in tomatoes, including juice (if from a can), and cook over medium heat. Stir in sugar and continue to cook, stirring occasionally, until sauce thickens, about 10 minutes. Serve with beef or pork.

MAKES 1½ TO 2 CUPS

Salads

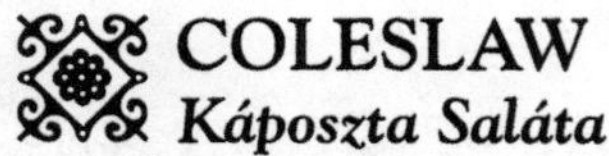

COLESLAW
Káposzta Saláta

5 cups thinly sliced cabbage
1 cup grated carrot
½ cup finely chopped green pepper
1 teaspoon salt
½ cup grated onion

Dressing

1 tablespoon sugar
½ teaspoon dry mustard
4 tablespoons white vinegar
2 tablespoons vegetable oil
2 teaspoons orange juice

In a large bowl, combine cabbage, carrot, green pepper, salt, and onion.

In a small bowl, combine sugar, dry mustard, vinegar, oil, and orange juice. Pour this mixture over the vegetables in the larger bowl and chill 3 hours.

Makes 6 cups

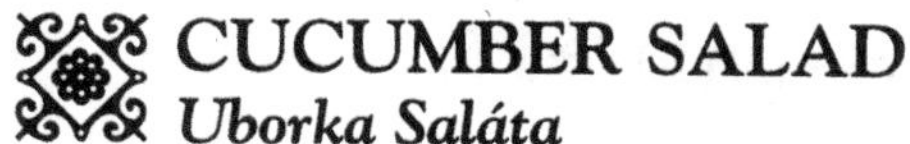

CUCUMBER SALAD
Uborka Saláta

This salad is crisp and cool. Its lightness complements most of the hearty, Hungarian meat entrees. Tip: Buy the cucumbers used for pickling. They are crispier and have smaller seeds than the larger cucumbers we use in salads.

3 large cucumbers, peeled
1½ teaspoons salt
3 tablespoons white vinegar
3 tablespoons water
½ teaspoon sugar
¼ teaspoon black pepper
½ teaspoon Hungarian paprika
1 onion, sliced thin

Slice cucumbers into thin rounds. Sprinkle with salt, mix lightly and let stand for 30 minutes. In another bowl, combine vinegar, water, sugar, pepper, paprika, and onions.

Squeeze excess moisture from cucumber slices, a handful at a time, and place into the vinegar mixture. Toss thoroughly; refrigerate 1 to 2 hours.

SERVES 4 TO 6

CUCUMBER SALAD WITH SOUR CREAM
Tejfölős Uborka Saláta

3 large cucumbers, peeled
1½ teaspoons salt
1 tablespoon white vinegar
1 cup sour cream

Thinly slice cucumbers. Sprinkle with salt; let stand 30 minutes. Stir vinegar into the sour cream. Squeeze excess moisture from cucumbers. Place into a bowl; add sour cream mixture and mix well. Refrigerate about an hour.

SERVES 4 TO 6

SOUR CREAM POTATO SALAD
Tejfölős Krumplisaláta

5 hard-boiled eggs, peeled
8 white rose potatoes, cooked and peeled
3 stalks celery, sliced thin
1 medium onion, chopped fine
1 teaspoon salt
¼ teaspoon black pepper
2 cups sour cream
¼ cup white vinegar
2 teaspoons sugar
Paprika for garnish

Chop 4 eggs and reserve 1 for garnish. Cut potatoes into 1-inch cubes or ¼-inch slices and place into a large bowl with celery, onion, and chopped eggs. Sprinkle salt and pepper over all and mix.

In a small bowl, blend sour cream, vinegar, and sugar and stir into the potato mixture. If desired, add more salt. Slice the reserved egg and spread slices over top of salad. Sprinkle with paprika and cover bowl with plastic wrap; let chill in the refrigerator for about 3 hours.

MAKES 3 TO 4 QUARTS

WARM HUNGARIAN POTATO SALAD
Meleg Krumplisaláta

The sour cream sauce is excellent over any cooked vegetables, especially broccoli, cauliflower, or green beans.

6 medium red or white rose potatoes, boiled, peeled, and sliced
3 hard-boiled eggs, sliced
3 tablespoons butter
6 green onions, sliced thin (include the greens)
1 cup sour cream
Salt
Pepper
1 tablespoon chopped fresh parsley

Place potatoes and eggs into a large bowl.

In a small saucepan, melt butter and sauté onions for 5 minutes, stirring occasionally. Add sour cream and stir.

Pour sauce over potatoes and eggs. Salt and pepper to taste; mix in parsley.

SERVES 6

WILTED LETTUCE SALAD
Forrázott Saláta

The lettuce will be limp and have the texture of a cooked vegetable. Garlic and bacon enhance the dressing's sweet and sour flavor.

4 slices bacon
2 tablespoons sugar
4 tablespoons water
4 tablespoons white vinegar
2 cloves garlic, minced
¼ teaspoon salt
1 head iceberg lettuce, cut into 6 wedges

Fry bacon and drain on paper towels.

Combine sugar, water, vinegar, garlic, and salt in a small saucepan and bring to a boil; remove from heat. Place lettuce wedges into a serving bowl, and pour vinegar dressing over all the pieces. Crumble bacon and distribute evenly over wedges. Allow the salad to set 15 minutes before serving.

SERVES 6

Soups

"Soup boiled is soup spoiled, so simmer your soup gently."
— Grandma Nagy

My comfort food was and still is Grandma Nagy's chicken noodle soup. Our family tradition was to serve it every Sunday with egg noodles made from scratch just a few days earlier. Grandma, Aunt Ethel, and Mother took turns staying home to cook the big pot of soup while the rest of the family went to church. On our return, the aroma of carrots, celery, onions, and fresh parsley simmering with the chicken drew us to the kitchen and enveloped us like a warm hug of welcome.

This weekly ritual began on Saturday when Grandma went to the chicken market to pick out a stewing hen for her large family. To ensure absolute freshness, Grandma took the hen home, killed it in the backyard, eviscerated it, then plunged it into boiling water to loosen its feathers for plucking. A 1932 cookbook belonging to Mother has a "how to" section that describes a method for killing poultry that would shock today's urban dwellers: "It is only humane to stun the bird before killing it. After hitting the bird on the head, bend its neck back and cut the throat with a sharp knife. The simplest way, of course, is to chop off the head with a meat axe."

Every part of the chicken was used (except the head) for soup. I continue to use the neck, liver, heart, and gizzard when making soup or gravy. Another delicacy (to our tastes) is chicken feet. Once sold abundantly, they are difficult to find except during holidays or in ethnic markets. The bones and cartilage deepen the soup flavor, and what fun it is to suck every drop of moisture from the cooked feet. My non-Hungarian friends find this practice repulsive so I never indulge when they are in my kitchen on a soup day.

Mother sometimes made the chicken perform double duty by roasting the same chicken she cooked in the soup pot. For us children, a special treat was the stuffed eggshells cooked right in the soup. Eggs used for the bread stuffing were carefully broken so that three-fourths of each shell remained intact. Mother then filled the shells with the stuffing she made for the chicken and put them into the soup pot to cook. In less than an hour the eggs were ready for us to spoon the filling out of the shells and straight into our mouths.

Tureen of chicken soup.

CHICKEN: FROM SOUP TO ROAST

One stuffed chicken makes a rich soup and a crispy roast. The trick to this recipe is not to overcook the chicken while in the broth, nor allow the bird to dry out while in the oven.

1 roasting chicken, 4½ to 5 pounds
Salt and pepper
3½ cups bread stuffing (page 106)
4 quarts water
2 medium onions, cut into halves
4 large stalks celery, cut into thirds
6 large carrots, cut into halves
½ green pepper, seeds removed
1 can (14.5 ounces) cut tomatoes, including juices
1 small cabbage, cut into wedges
1 tablespoon salt (or to taste)
12 to 15 sprigs Italian parsley, tied in a bundle
½ teaspoon peppercorns
Pinch of saffron
16-ounce package thin egg noodles

Seasoning Mixture

½ teaspoon salt
¼ teaspoon black pepper
1 teaspoon paprika

Wash chicken inside and out; blot dry. Lightly salt and pepper cavity. Prepare stuffing. Fill chicken cavity loosely, putting any excess stuffing into an ovenproof dish to be baked with the bird. Close opening with skewers or string.

Place chicken into a 10-quart soup pot. Add water; bring to a gentle boil. Skim foam as it bubbles to the surface.

When foam stops surfacing, reduce heat to medium and add onions, celery, carrots, green pepper, tomatoes, cabbage, salt, parsley, peppercorns, and saffron. Cover and simmer gently 40 to 50 minutes. Turn off heat.

Preheat oven to 425 degrees 15 minutes before soup has completed cooking.

Cook the noodles according to package directions, drain, and set aside.

Remove chicken from the broth and place in a shallow roasting pan, breast side up. Combine seasoning mixture ingredients and rub over top of chicken.

Skim any fat from the surface of the soup and use it to baste the chicken. Place chicken and any excess dressing into oven and roast until the chicken is a rich, brown color (15 to 20 minutes). If chicken is browning too rapidly, reduce oven temperature to 400 degrees. Use a meat thermometer to determine if meat is cooked thoroughly.

Strain soup and put clear broth into a soup tureen; add cooked noodles. For the second course, place cooked carrots, onions, and cabbage on a serving plate. Remove stuffing from the chicken and place on one end of a large, warm serving platter. Cut the chicken into serving pieces and place on the platter with the stuffing.

Baked yams and cucumber salad round out this royal meal.

SERVES 6 TO 8

BEEF SOUP WITH VEGETABLES
Hús Leves Zöldséggel

This long-simmering soup yields not only a first course meal, but a second course as well. Vegetables are cooked whole and served with the meat. Our family's preference for this soup is small, square-shaped noodles.

3 pounds beef (chuck roast or thick slices of chuck steak)
3 quarts water
2 tablespoons salt
1 teaspoon peppercorns
6 peeled carrots
4 stalks celery, washed with leaves intact
1 cup chopped tomatoes
2 onions, peeled and left whole
15 to 20 sprigs Italian parsley, tied in a bundle
½ head cabbage, cut into wedges
3 large potatoes, peeled and cut into halves
3 to 4 cups cooked egg noodles, homemade (page 83) or store bought

Wash meat, cut into 6 pieces and place in a 6-quart pot. Add water and bring to a boil. Skim foam as it rises to the surface. Continue boiling until foam no longer surfaces. Reduce heat; add salt, peppercorns, carrots, celery, tomatoes, onions, and parsley. Cover and simmer 2 to 2½ hours.

Add cabbage and potatoes; cover and simmer 20 to 30 minutes, or until potatoes are cooked. Remove meat and vegetables from pot; discard parsley. Strain soup; discard peppercorns.

Combine soup and cooked noodles in a tureen.

For your second course, place pieces of meat and cooked vegetables on a serving platter.

Horseradish relish (page 38) goes well with the beef.

SERVES 6 TO 8

CABBAGE SOUP
Káposztás Leves

Thick slices of pumpernickel or rye bread are ideal with this soup.

3 pounds smoked ham hocks
2 bay leaves
1 whole onion
1 teaspoon peppercorns
3 quarts water
1 head cabbage, chopped
1 tomato, chopped
1 teaspoon vinegar

Over medium heat, cover and cook ham hocks, bay leaves, onion, and peppercorns in water for 2 hours.

Remove onion and bay leaves; discard. Remove ham hocks from the water; when cool enough to handle, cut meat off the bones and chop into bite-size pieces. Skim fat off surface of soup. Discard bones and return meat to the pot. Place cabbage and tomato into the pot and cook until the cabbage is tender (10 to 15 minutes). Stir in the vinegar.

SERVES 8 TO 10

CHERRY SOUP
Cseresznye Leves

The purist would use fresh sour cherries for this soup. However, since these are difficult to find, canned sour cherries may be substituted. Cherry soup is delicious whether eaten warm, at room temperature, or chilled.

- 1 can (16 ounces) sour pitted cherries, including juice, or 1½ pounds fresh sour cherries, washed and pitted
- 3 cups water
- 1-inch cinnamon stick
- 1 tablespoon sugar
- ¼ teaspoon salt
- 1 tablespoon flour
- 1 cup sour cream

Bring cherries and water to boil. Add cinnamon stick, sugar, and salt; stir and keep at a low boil until cherries are soft (if using fresh cherries).

Blend flour into sour cream; gradually add to soup. Lower heat and simmer, uncovered, 10 minutes. Add more sugar if needed.

SERVES 4

CHICKEN VEGETABLE SOUP WITH DUMPLINGS

Becsinált Leves Galuskával

My mother-in-law used chicken backs for this easy-to-make soup. I find chicken backs much too fatty in today's markets and substitute other chicken parts, adding chicken bouillon if stronger depth of flavor is needed.

2 to 3 pounds chicken parts
3 quarts water
1½ cups chopped carrots
1½ cups chopped celery
2 kohlrabi, peeled and diced, or 2 cups chopped cabbage
1 cup chopped onion
2 teaspoons salt (reduce to 1 teaspoon if bouillon is used)
¼ teaspoon black pepper
10 sprigs Italian parsley, washed and tied in a bundle
1 chicken bouillon cube, optional
Liver dumplings (page 82)

Place chicken parts and water in a 6-quart soup pot; bring to a boil. Skim foam as it rises to the top.

Lower heat to medium, cover, and cook 20 minutes; add carrots, celery, kohlrabi (or cabbage), onion, salt, pepper, and parsley. Simmer until chicken is tender, about 20 minutes. Add bouillon, if needed.

Remove chicken from the soup; cut the meat from the bones and dice into bite-size pieces. Return meat to the soup and discard bones (unless you like to chew on them). Add cooked dumplings to the soup. Dumpling batter may be spoon-dropped directly into gently boiling soup during the last 10 minutes of cooking.

SERVES 6 TO 8

CREAMED CAULIFLOWER SOUP
Tejfeles Karfiolleves

1 large head cauliflower, trimmed
1 cup chopped onion
2 stalks celery, sliced thin
2 tablespoons vegetable oil
6 cups chicken stock or broth
1 tablespoon coarsely chopped Italian parsley

Roux
2 tablespoons butter
2 tablespoons flour
¼ cup cold water
¼ teaspoon white pepper
1 cup sour cream

Break cauliflower into small florets and set aside.

In a 4-quart saucepan, sauté onions and celery in oil until onions are soft. Add cauliflower and broth, cover and cook on low heat for 8 minutes, or until cauliflower is crisp-tender, not soft.

Make the roux while cauliflower cooks. Melt the butter in an 8-inch skillet; add flour. Stir constantly while cooking on medium heat until flour is golden brown (about 10 minutes).

Add the cold water, stir until smooth. Add pepper and sour cream. Mix well and stir into soup pot. Simmer, uncovered, on medium for 5 minutes. Sprinkle with parsley just before serving.

Serves 6

CREAMED GREEN BEAN SOUP
Tejfeles Zöldbab Leves

Eat this soup hot on a cold, wintry day, or eat it cold on a sizzling summer afternoon or evening. I even like it for breakfast.

1 pound fresh string beans, cut into 2-inch pieces
1½ quarts water
1 teaspoon salt
2 tablespoons solid shortening
2 tablespoons flour
¼ teaspoon white or black pepper
½ teaspoon Hungarian paprika
¼ cup water
1 cup sour cream

Over medium heat, cook beans, covered, in 1½ quarts salted water until tender, but not soft, about 15 minutes. In a skillet, melt shortening and brown flour until it is the color of honey. Add pepper, paprika, and ¼ cup water to the skillet. Stir until smooth, and blend in sour cream. Pour this mixture into the simmering beans, stirring as you pour. Continue to simmer over medium heat 5 to 8 minutes as broth thickens.

SERVES 4 TO 5

NEW WORLD CREAMED GREEN BEAN SOUP

I learned to make this lighter version from my mother-in-law. Because this is one of my family's favorites, I make a big batch—enough for plenty of leftovers. Cut the recipe in half if it makes too much for your family.

2 pounds fresh string beans, cut into 2-inch pieces
2½ quarts water
1 tablespoon salt
1¼ cups low-fat milk
¾ cup flour
1 egg, beaten with a fork
½ cup sour cream
8 to 10 sprigs Italian parsley, leaves only
1 tablespoon white vinegar
1 cube chicken bouillon

Cook the beans in salted water as above until tender but not soft, about 15 minutes.

While the beans are cooking, pour milk into a medium bowl. Add flour and whisk until lumps disappear. In a small bowl, combine egg and sour cream; mix until smooth and add to the flour/milk mixture. If necessary, strain lumps through a sieve. Pour sour cream mixture into the pot of beans simmering on low-medium heat, stirring constantly. Add parsley, vinegar, and bouillon; stir and continue to simmer on low-medium heat for 8 to 10 minutes, until liquid thickens.

Variations:

Add diced potatoes during the last 10 minutes of cooking.
Add cauliflower during last 10 minutes of cooking.
Add cooked, diced giblets.
Add sliced, smoked sausage.

SERVES 8 TO 10

KOHLRABI SOUP
Karalábé Leves

How do you tell a kohlrabi from a turnip? Well, the kohlrabi looks and cooks like a turnip, but, uncooked, it tastes like a radish or the crisp core of raw cabbage. In fact, this vegetable gets its name from the German word for cabbage (*kohl*) and the Latin name for turnip (*rapa*). It looks like a root, but actually is a swollen stem, and, if picked when it is about the size of a tennis ball, tastes much sweeter than a turnip. One way to enjoy kohlrabi is to eat it raw as a snack. Remove the leaves, peel and slice it. For extra crispness, put slices in water and place in the refrigerator for an hour. When ready to eat, drain off the water. I like to season the slices with salt and pepper. With a sandwich, this is better than potato chips. Hungarians incorporate kohlrabi in soups, as it combines well with other vegetables and most meats. If you can't find kohlrabi in your market, substitute ½ head chopped cabbage. This is an easy basic soup recipe. If you wish to thicken the soup, use the roux recipe on page 67.

2 quarts water
2 teaspoons salt
2 cups chopped carrots
3 cups chopped celery
1 cup chopped onion
3 or 5 kohlrabi, leaves removed, peeled, and diced
1 parsley root with leaves, or 10 to 15 sprigs Italian parsley, tied in a bundle
1 teaspoon peppercorn

Combine all ingredients. Bring to a boil; reduce heat to simmer. Cover and cook 20 to 30 minutes, or until vegetables are tender.

SERVES 6 TO 8

ROUX
Rántás

Hungarian cooks like to add body and color to their soups. This is done by making a roux, a blend of equal amounts of flour and fat cooked together. This method dates back several centuries and was introduced to Hungarian cuisine through the French influence.

- 2 tablespoons lard, margarine, butter, or vegetable shortening
- 2 tablespoons flour
- 1 teaspoon paprika
- 1 cup broth from cooking pot

In a heavy skillet, melt the lard over medium-low heat. Add the flour and stir with a whisk or a wooden spoon until flour is the color of light brown sugar. Do not hurry this process, for too much heat will burn the flour and produce a bitter taste. Add paprika and broth, stirring until thick and smooth. Pour into simmering soup pot; continue to cook 5 more minutes.

This will thicken 2 quarts of soup.

New World Version

Mix 2 tablespoons flour with 1 cup liquid. Liquid could be water, milk (for a sour cream-based soup), or cooled broth from the soup. Blend until lumps disappear and pour into simmering pot; continue to cook 5 more minutes.

LENTIL SOUP WITH SAUSAGE
Lencse Leves Kolbásszal

1 ham bone or ½ pound Hungarian smoked sausage, cut into ½-inch slices
1 quart water
1 quart chicken broth
½ pound dry lentils, washed
½ teaspoon salt
1 onion, finely chopped
1 cup diced carrots
2 stalks celery, diced
2 tablespoons flour
2 tablespoons butter, melted
1 teaspoon paprika
1 cup cold water
1 tablespoon white vinegar

Place ham bone or sausage into 1 quart water and add broth. Add lentils, salt, onion, carrots, and celery. Cook, covered, on medium heat until lentils and vegetables are tender, about 45 minutes.

In a skillet brown flour in butter; add paprika and cook another minute.

Add 1 cup cold water to flour mixture and cook until mixture thickens, stirring constantly. Add to lentil broth and continue to simmer 5 minutes longer. Stir in the vinegar.

Before serving, remove ham bone from soup and cool slightly. Cut meat from the bone, cube it, and return to soup. Discard the bone or give it to your favorite dog.

SERVES 6 TO 8

NAVY BEAN AND SAUSAGE SOUP
Bableves Kolbásszal

Beans must be soaked to make them soft and digestible. If you can't soak the beans overnight, use the quick-soak method: cover beans with water, bring to a boil, boiling for 2 minutes. Turn off heat and let beans set, covered, for 1 hour. Discard water and rinse beans before cooking. This method holds true for all legumes with the exception of dry peas and lentils, which need no soaking.

½ pound navy beans (small, white beans)
2 quarts water
½ pound Hungarian smoked sausage, cut in ¼-inch slices
1 teaspoon salt
¼ teaspoon pepper
½ cup diced onion
½ cup diced celery
1 cup chopped carrots
1 cup chopped tomatoes
2 bay leaves
10 sprigs Italian parsley, tied in a bundle
1 teaspoon white vinegar
Pinched noodles (page 87), or 8-ounce package noodles

ROUX
2 tablespoons shortening
2 tablespoons flour
1 teaspoon paprika

Wash beans; cover with cold water, and soak overnight, or use the quick-soak method described above.

Drain and rinse beans and place into a 6-quart pot with 2 quarts water, sausage, salt, pepper, onion, celery, carrots, tomatoes, bay leaves, and parsley. Heat to boiling; reduce heat. Cover and simmer 1 hour. Add vinegar.

In a small skillet, heat shortening, add flour, and stir until golden brown. Stir in paprika. Gradually add roux to soup and simmer 10 minutes. Add noodles and simmer another 10 minutes.

SERVES 4 TO 6

SOUR CREAM POTATO SOUP
Tejfeles Krumpli Leves

Adding a chicken bouillon cube enhances the flavor of this rich soup, once considered peasants' fare.

- 4 large, peeled and diced potatoes (new or white rose potatoes provide the firmness needed)
- 1 onion, chopped
- 4 cups water
- 1 chicken bouillon cube
- ½ teaspoon salt
- 2 tablespoons butter
- 2 tablespoons flour
- 1 cup cold water
- ¼ teaspoon white pepper, optional
- 1 cup sour cream
- 1 tablespoon chopped Italian parsley

Combine potatoes, onion, 4 cups water, bouillon cube, and salt in a 4-quart cooking pot. Cook on medium heat 15 to 20 minutes, or until potatoes are tender.

In a skillet, melt the butter, add flour and brown slightly. Add 1 cup cold water and stir until smooth. A wooden spoon or wire whisk does the job well. Pour this mixture into the cooked potatoes while stirring the broth; boil gently for 3 minutes. Broth will thicken slightly. Add pepper, if desired.

Add sour cream. (To keep sour cream from curdling, remove 1 cup broth from soup, place it in a small bowl and allow to cool slightly. Add sour cream to the cooled broth and mix well before stirring it back into the pot).

Garnish with parsley.

SERVES 6

NEW WORLD CREAMY POTATO SOUP

2 cups chicken broth
1 small onion, chopped
4 medium potatoes, peeled and diced (baking potatoes work well)
2 tablespoons butter or margarine
2 tablespoons flour
1 cup low-fat milk
½ teaspoon dried dill
1 tablespoon vinegar
Salt to taste
1 tablespoon chopped parsley or ½ teaspoon paprika

In a 4-quart saucepan, combine broth, onion, and potatoes. Bring mixture to a boil. Reduce heat; cover and simmer for 15 minutes, or until potatoes are tender.

Place half of the soup into a food processor or blender. Process until smooth. Pour processed potatoes into a bowl. Repeat with remaining half of potatoes. (If more texture is desired, process only half of the potato mixture).

Using the same saucepan, melt the butter and stir in the flour. Slowly add milk. Cook until mixture is thick and bubbly, stirring constantly. Add the potato mixture, dill, and vinegar. Add salt if needed. Stir until soup is heated through.

Serve warm in bowls with parsley or paprika.

SERVES 4

PORK OR BEEF NECK BONE SOUP
Nyak Csont Leves, Disznó vagy Marha

2½ pounds pork or beef neck bones
4 quarts water
1 tablespoon salt
1 peeled onion, left whole
¼ teaspoon peppercorns
3 stalks celery, cut into thirds, crosswise
4 large carrots, cut into halves, crosswise
3 cloves garlic, whole
½ green pepper, seeds removed
1 can (16 ounces) whole or diced tomatoes, with juice
1 head cabbage, cut into 6 wedges
10 sprigs Italian parsley, tied in a bundle
4 cups cooked egg noodles

Rinse bones and place in an 8-quart pot. Add water and bring to a boil. Remove foam as it rises to the surface. When no more foam bubbles up, reduce heat and add the salt, onion, and peppercorns. Cover and simmer 1½ hours.

Add celery, carrots, garlic, green pepper, tomatoes, cabbage, and parsley.

Cover pot and bring broth to a boil. Lower the heat to medium and cook partially uncovered for 20 minutes, or until vegetables are tender.

Remove neck bones, carrots, and cabbage. Strain broth; pour into soup bowls filled with ½ cup of cooked egg noodles.

Serve carrots and cabbage with the neck bones.

Meat cooked in this manner (in liquid) is sometimes served with a sauce such as tomato, cherry, or horseradish. See pages 43, 40, 38.

SERVES 6 TO 8

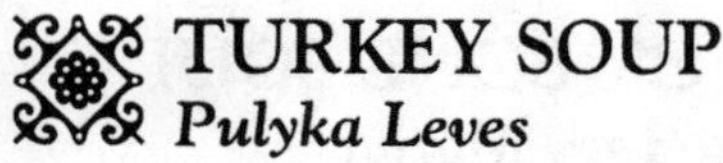

TURKEY SOUP
Pulyka Leves

To enjoy turkey soup you needn't wait for Thanksgiving's turkey bones.

Turkey breast, about 3 pounds
1 to 1½ pounds turkey necks
4 quarts water
2 teaspoons salt
2 cups chopped onions
2 cups carrots, cut into half-inch rounds
2 cups chopped celery
1 can (14½ ounces) peeled, diced tomatoes
3 cups chopped cabbage
½ teaspoon pepper
1 chicken bouillon cube
10 sprigs Italian parsley, tied in a bundle
8 to 10 threads saffron, optional

In an 8-quart pot, combine turkey breast, necks, water, and salt. Bring to a boil over high heat. Skim foam that rises to the surface and discard.

Lower heat to medium-low, cover and simmer 1 to 1½ hours, or until breast is tender. Add onions, carrots, celery, tomatoes, cabbage, pepper, bouillon cube, parsley, and saffron.

Cover and continue to simmer 20 minutes. Remove turkey breast from the pot. Cut the meat from breastbone and dice into small chunks. Return meat to soup and mix into cooked vegetables. Soup is now ready to be served.

Reserve turkey necks for diners who consider this a delicacy.

SERVES 8 TO 10

Biscuits, Dumplings, and Noodles

HOMEMADE CRACKLINGS
Tepertö

Pork cracklings, used in biscuit and pasta recipes usually can be purchased at European markets. If cracklings are not available, use this method of making your own.

1 pound slab bacon
3 tablespoons water

Cut the skin off the bacon leaving a layer of fat about ½ inch thick. Cut the skin into 2-inch squares and put into a heavy skillet with water. Cook slowly until all the fat is rendered. Remove the crackling from the skillet and drain on paper towels; chop fine. Save the fat for pies and other recipes.

Note: If you can't find bacon slabs, use 6 to 8 slices thick bacon, frying until all fat is rendered.

MAKES ABOUT 1 CUP.

CRACKLING BISCUITS
Tepertős Pogácsa

3 cups all-purpose flour
1 teaspoon salt
1 tablespoon butter, melted
½ cup cracklings (page 76)
2 egg yolks, at room temperature, beaten slightly
1 cup sour cream, at room temperature
1 yeast cake or dry envelope yeast, dissolved in ¼ cup warm milk

In a large bowl, mix flour, salt, butter, and cracklings by hand; set aside. Put 1 egg yolk and sour cream into yeast mixture and stir gently. Add this combination to the flour mixture and mix well. Let the dough rise in a warm place until double in size, 30 to 45 minutes.

Preheat oven to 350 degrees.

Place dough on a floured board and knead about 10 times always turning your dough. Roll out to 1-inch thickness and cut with a round 3-inch cookie cutter. Place biscuits on a greased cookie sheet and brush with egg yolk.

Bake about 30 minutes or until golden brown.

MAKES 20 BISCUITS

Eggs, flour, water.

QUICK HUNGARIAN BISCUITS
Gyors Magyar Pogácsa

2 cups flour
1 teaspoon salt
½ teaspoon baking powder
½ teaspoon baking soda
½ cup solid vegetable shortening
¾ cup buttermilk
½ cup cracklings (page 76)
1 egg yolk, beaten, optional

Preheat oven to 350 degrees.

Combine and mix the flour, salt, baking powder, and baking soda in a large mixing bowl. Add the shortening. Using a pastry blender or two knives, work shortening into the dry ingredients until the mixture resembles the texture of oatmeal.

Add buttermilk and cracklings; stir with a fork just until the dough forms a mass. Turn the dough out on a lightly floured board. Knead about 12 times.

Roll out to a 2-inch thickness and cut into circles with a round 3-inch cookie cutter.

Place on a greased cookie sheet. With a fork, press a tic-tac-toe design on each cookie (children love to do this). For a shiny glaze, brush biscuits with a beaten egg yolk. Bake 25 to 30 minutes or until golden brown.

MAKES ABOUT 15 BISCUITS.

DUMPLINGS
Galuska

5 quarts water plus ½ cup water
3 teaspoons salt
2½ cups flour
2 eggs, slightly beaten
¼ cup melted butter, optional

Bring to boil 5 quarts water with 2 teaspoons salt. Meanwhile, combine the flour with 1 teaspoon salt and set aside. In a medium bowl, mix the eggs and ½ cup water. Gradually add the flour/salt mixture to the eggs, beating with a spoon until smooth. Batter should be thick like bread dough. Add more flour if needed. Drop by spoonfuls into salted boiling water. The dumplings will double in size as they rise to the surface. Boil gently 5 to 8 minutes, stirring occasionally. Drain dumplings and place in a warm bowl. Toss with butter if desired.

MAKES 3 CUPS DUMPLINGS

Dumplings.

LIVER DUMPLINGS
Májas Galuska

1 egg, beaten
1 tablespoon butter, melted
1 tablespoon water
4 chicken livers, ground, or chopped fine
3 tablespoons bread crumbs
3 tablespoons flour
½ teaspoon salt
1 teaspoon finely chopped parsley

Combine egg, butter, and water. Add chicken livers, bread crumbs, flour, salt, and parsley; mix well.

Drop by teaspoonfuls into medium pot of slowly simmering soup. Cook, uncovered, until all the dumplings float to the top (about 8 minutes).

Liver dumplings greatly enhance vegetable or poultry soups.

MAKES ENOUGH DUMPLINGS FOR 2 QUARTS OF SOUP

EGG NOODLES
Tojásos Tészta

I used to watch my mother use her special sharp knife to cut dough into the narrowest threads possible. She did this with the speed and confidence of a professional chef. Mother sometimes cut the dough into tiny squares. Our family preference was to use the thin noodles for chicken soup and the square noodles for beef or pork soup. For those who do not wish to make noodles from scratch, packaged egg noodles can be found in the pasta or international section of grocery stores.

2 cups flour
2 eggs
2 tablespoons water
Flour for dusting pastry board

Measure flour onto a pastry board; make a well. Beat eggs, add the water and mix; pour egg mixture into the well. With your hands, blend the egg mixture into the flour until dough forms a ball. Knead the dough using the heel of your palm, until the dough is smooth, 10 to 15 minutes. Sprinkle the pastry board with flour as needed. Cover the dough with a bowl for 15 minutes. Lightly flour the board and roll the dough out until it is very thin. (Mother used an 18-inch rolling pin for this, but a standard-length rolling pin will do the job).

Allow the dough to dry about 15 minutes (longer, if it is a rainy day). Cut into 3-inch strips. Stack 5 strips at a time, one atop the other and cut crosswise into fine strings.

Cook the noodles in salted water for about 5 minutes, or until noodles are tender. Drain and rinse.

If the noodles are not to be cooked immediately, spread them out in a single layer on a flat surface and allow to dry completely. Once dry, the noodles may be stored in an airtight container.

MAKES ENOUGH NOODLES FOR 3 QUARTS OF SOUP

BAKED NOODLES
Rakott Tészta

This is usually enjoyed as a dessert. To serve as a main dish, omit the sugar.

4 quarts water
1 tablespoon salt
16 ounces wide noodles
¼ pound butter, melted
2 cups cottage cheese
½ cup sugar
¼ cup sliced almonds

Preheat oven to 350 degrees.

Bring water and salt to a boil. Add noodles and boil, stirring occasionally, until noodles are tender (about 8 minutes). Drain and rinse with cold water. When noodles are thoroughly drained, place ¼ into a 2-quart buttered baking dish. Pour ¼ of the butter over noodles, spread ¼ cheese and sprinkle ¼ sugar over this first layer. Continue the remaining 3 layers in this manner. Sprinkle almonds over the top. Bake for 30 minutes. Serve hot.

SERVES 6

Variation:

Substitute 1 pound coarsely ground walnuts for the cottage cheese.

CABBAGE AND NOODLES WITH BACON

Káposztás Tészta

1 large head cabbage, shredded
1 teaspoon salt
½ pound thick-sliced, smoked bacon
12 ounces wide noodles

Place cabbage into a bowl and sprinkle with salt; let stand 30 minutes.

In a large skillet, fry bacon slices until brown; set aside. Cut into pieces when cool. Remove 3 tablespoons bacon fat from skillet and reserve.

Squeeze moisture from the cabbage and cook in hot fat remaining in the skillet. (Discard any fat that exceeds 3 remaining tablespoons).

Stir frequently while the cabbage is frying, uncovered. Cook until the cabbage is tender and slightly brown, about 30 minutes.

In a large pot, cook noodles in salt water according to package directions. Drain; return noodles to cooking pot; mix in reserved fat, bacon pieces, and fried cabbage. Serve hot as a side dish.

SERVES 5 TO 6

NEW WORLD VERSION

Substitute ½ pound smoked turkey sausage, diced, for the bacon. Fry the cabbage in 3 tablespoons vegetable oil.

NOODLES WITH COTTAGE CHEESE
Túrós Tészta

Noodles with cottage cheese provide a tasty side dish for poultry and meats.

12 ounces wide noodles
4 quarts water
1 teaspoon salt
4 slices thick bacon
2 cups cottage cheese
2 tablespoons sour cream
¼ teaspoon pepper

Cook noodles in salted water according to package directions. Drain and set aside.

Fry bacon until crisp. Drain on paper towels and chop coarsely.

Return noodles to cooking pan. Add cottage cheese, sour cream, and pepper to pan; mix well. Stir in bacon.

SERVES 4 TO 6

NEW WORLD VERSION

Omit the bacon and reduce sour cream to 1 tablespoon.

PINCHED NOODLES
Csipetke Tészta

Pinched noodles are cooked directly in vegetable or bean soups during the last 10 minutes of cooking time. These noodles are larger in size than egg barley, but not as large as dumplings made for stews like goulash or chicken paprikas.

1 cup flour
½ teaspoon salt
1 egg
2 teaspoons water

Place flour and salt into a medium bowl. Make a well in the center of the flour. Add egg and water; mix with hands until flour has absorbed the egg and water and forms a ball. Place dough on a board and knead about 15 times using heel of both hands. Dough will be smooth and feel like a baby's bottom.

Flatten the dough, using your hands or a rolling pin, to ½-inch thickness. Slice into ¼-inch strips. Pinch ¼-inch pieces from the strips (about the size of peas) directly into gently boiling soup. Cook, uncovered, 8 to 10 minutes.

SERVES 6

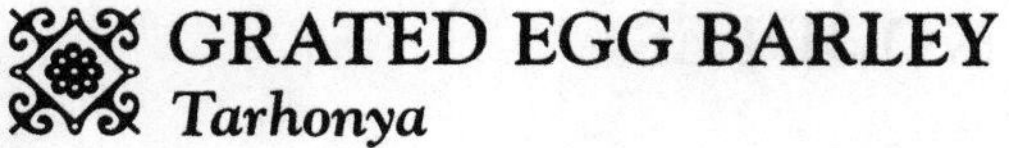

GRATED EGG BARLEY
Tarhonya

Egg barley can be purchased at the grocery store in 7-ounce or 12-ounce packages, or you can easily make this recipe.

1½ cups flour
¼ teaspoon salt
1 egg

In a medium bowl, sift flour and salt. Add egg and mix thoroughly to form a hard dough. It is easier to mix by hand. Grate through large holes of grater or push through a ricer over a pastry board. Spread out thinly on board to dry. Store in a covered container until ready to cook.

MAKES 1½ CUPS

BROWNED EGG BARLEY
Piritott Tarhonya

Egg barley is an excellent substitute for potatoes and pairs well with chicken and pork.

1 tablespoon butter
1 cup dry egg barley
2 cups chicken broth

Melt butter in a medium skillet. Add barley and brown for 5 to 7 minutes, stirring to brown evenly.

Add broth, cover, and bring to a boil. Reduce heat; cover and cook 20 minutes or until barley is tender. Noodles will double in volume.

SERVES 4

Poultry

BREADED FRIED CHICKEN
Kirántott Csirke

In the small town of Rabaszentandrás, where my mother was born, relatives still raise their own vegetables and chickens. On my first visit to the village, I was greeted so enthusiastically I felt like the prodigal daughter who finally came home. Even though I arrived unannounced, I was expected to stay for dinner. I could smell breaded chicken frying in the kitchen while we visited in the living room reminiscent of my grandparents' parlor at home. It, too, was used only for company. The chicken was the best I have ever tasted. In asking for their secret to cooking fried chicken (besides the advantage of fresh chicken plucked from the backyard), I was given two tips: 1.) Soak the chicken in cold, salted water for 30 to 60 minutes before coating with bread crumbs—this adds flavor and tenderizes the meat; 2.) After coating all the pieces, let chicken set for 30 minutes—this prevents the bread coating from coming off during frying.

- 1 fryer chicken, 3 pounds, disjointed (save the neck and giblets for soup)
- ¾ cup flour
- 1 teaspoon salt
- ½ teaspoon pepper
- 1 egg, slightly beaten
- ¼ cup milk
- 1½ cups fine dry bread crumbs
- 3 cups solid vegetable shortening

Soak chicken in enough salted water to cover all chicken parts for 30 to 60 minutes.

Combine flour, salt, and pepper in a shallow dish. Combine the egg and milk in another dish; spread bread crumbs into a third dish. (Pie pans are perfect for this step.)

Pat chicken parts dry with a paper towel; cover each piece with the flour mixture, then the egg mixture. Roll each chicken part in the bread crumbs, pressing the crumbs onto the chicken with your fingers. Let chicken set for 30 minutes.

In a deep, heavy skillet, large enough to hold all chicken parts in one layer, heat shortening over medium heat to a temperature of 350 degrees; or use the bread crumb test: when a pinch of bread crumbs sizzles in the oil, it is ready for the chicken.

Fry chicken on medium heat until browned on all sides, 35 to 40 minutes. Lower heat if chicken is browning too fast, but keep it hot and sizzling. Add more oil as needed.

Drain chicken on paper towels and keep warm until ready to serve.

SERVES 4

NEW WORLD VERSION

Instead of deep-frying chicken, reduce shortening to ¼ cup; brown parts quickly on medium-high, transfer to a baking pan, and bake in 350 degree oven 25 to 30 minutes. Test with a fork for tenderness.

CHICKEN LIVERS WITH ONIONS
Csirke Máj Hagymával

For a change in breakfast fare, try this recipe with eggs and toast, or, serve it as a light supper.

½ to ¾ pound chicken livers
2 tablespoons unsalted butter
2 cups sliced onions
1 teaspoon salt
¼ teaspoon pepper
1 teaspoon paprika
¼ cup white wine

Rinse chicken livers, drain, and set aside.

Melt butter over medium heat. Add onions and livers; sauté, uncovered, until liver and onions brown slightly, about 10 minutes. Add salt, pepper, paprika, and wine. Reduce heat; cover and cook 10 minutes longer.

SERVES 4

CHICKEN PAPRIKA
Chirke Paprikás

Once the technique for removing the fiery veins and seeds of red pepper was invented in Szeged, Hungary, in 1859, paprika was referred to as the "noble sweet rose." Used as a primary spice for seasoning meats, poultry, fish, and vegetables, the Hungarian cook keeps her pantry well stocked with paprika.

- 2 tablespoons vegetable oil
- 1 cup chopped onion
- 4 to 5 pounds disjointed chicken, visible fat removed, breast cut in half
- 1 tablespoon paprika
- 1 teaspoon black pepper
- 2 tablespoons salt
- 2 cups water
- 2 tablespoons flour
- ½ cup milk
- ½ cup sour cream, at room temperature

Heat oil; sauté onion until soft. Add chicken parts; season with paprika, pepper, and salt. Sauté chicken on one side, then turn until outsides of chicken parts are no longer pink. Add water; cover and simmer on low heat until chicken is tender (about 40 minutes).

To thicken broth, combine flour, milk, and sour cream. Beat with a wire whisk to eliminate lumps. Remove chicken from pot; bring broth to gentle boil on medium heat and pour in sour cream mixture, stirring continually until broth thickens. Reduce heat and simmer 5 minutes. Replace chicken and coat each piece with gravy. Heat through and serve with plain or liver dumplings (page 80, 82).

Baked yams and cucumber salad complement this classic recipe.

SERVES 4 TO 6

MOM'S CHICKEN AND RICE
Mama Rizses Csirkéje

2 tablespoons vegetable oil
1 cup chopped onion
1 cup chopped celery
1 cup chopped carrots
1 clove garlic, minced
1 chicken (3 to 4 pounds), disjointed (or use your favorite chicken parts)
2 teaspoons salt
½ teaspoon black pepper
2 teaspoons Hungarian paprika
3½ cups water
1½ cups rice (converted rice preferred)
10 sprigs fresh Italian parsley, chopped

In a large pot, heat oil; sauté onion, celery, carrots, and garlic until onions are soft.

Remove vegetables. Place chicken parts into the same pot. On medium heat cook both sides of each chicken part only until pink flesh turns white. Return vegetables to pot and sprinkle all with salt, pepper, and paprika. Add ½ cup water. Cover and simmer for 20 minutes.

Add remaining 3 cups water, mix in rice and bring to a boil. Reduce heat to low; cover and cook 20 minutes, or until rice and chicken are tender. Stir in parsley.

SERVES 4 TO 6

ROAST CHICKEN STUFFED WITH ONIONS, GARLIC, AND HERBS

Sült Csirke

Traditional bread stuffing is not needed here to provide flavor. Slivers of garlic placed under the skin give the chicken a fresh new taste.

1 (4-pound) whole chicken
2 tablespoons vegetable oil
3 onions, coarsely chopped
½ cup chopped fresh parsley
2 tablespoons chopped fresh basil
1 teaspoon salt
½ teaspoon black pepper
5 cloves garlic, peeled and slivered
Paprika

Remove visible fat from cavity; soak chicken in cold, salted water for 1 hour.

Preheat oven to 350 degrees

In a large skillet, heat oil over medium heat. Add onions and sauté 5 minutes. Add parsley, basil, salt, and pepper; stir and sauté 2 minutes longer. Set aside.

Drain and dry chicken with paper towels, inside and out. Pull skin away from both breasts and distribute slivers of 4 cloves evenly under the skin. Put remaining slivers into chicken's cavity.

Lightly rub salt and pepper into cavity before filling with onion mixture. Close cavity by sewing or using thin skewers. Season surface of chicken with salt, pepper, and paprika.

Place chicken in a large roasting pan breast up; roast, uncovered, for 60 to 70 minutes, occasionally basting chicken with its own juices. Chicken should be golden brown. Allow chicken to stand 10 minutes before carving. To make gravy from drippings, see page 99.

SERVES 4 TO 6

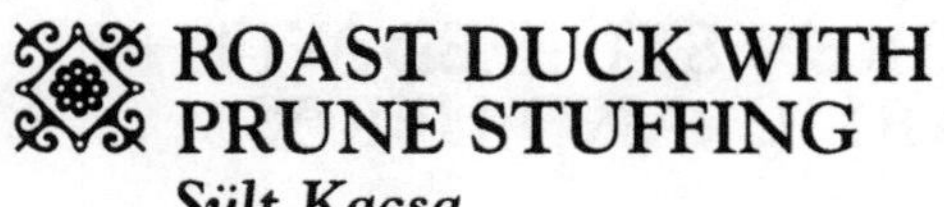

ROAST DUCK WITH PRUNE STUFFING

Sült Kacsa

The secret of cooking the typically fat duck is to begin roasting on very high heat, then turning the bird often, pouring off excess fat from the pan as it melts. The longer the duck roasts, the crisper the skin will become. Duck has no white meat so it is the perfect fowl for a family who fights over who gets the dark meat.

¼ pound pitted prunes
1 cup chopped onion
1 tablespoon vegetable oil
¼ pound lean ground pork
½ teaspoon salt
¼ teaspoon pepper
2 tablespoons chopped fresh parsley
1 (4½-to 5½-pound) duck

Soak prunes in water the day before. Drain and coarsely chop.

Preheat oven to 500 degrees.

In a medium skillet, sauté onion in oil until soft. Add pork, salt, and pepper; cook, stirring, until meat is no longer pink. Stir in prunes and parsley. Allow stuffing to cool.

Wash and dry the duck. Trim excess fat and skin from neck opening. Stuff cavity of duck with prune and pork mixture and truss (close cavity by sewing). Sprinkle duck with salt and pepper. Place in roasting pan, back side down. Roast until duck starts to brown, about 30 minutes.

Turn duck over onto its breast; reduce heat to 325 degrees. Roast 30 minutes. Discard fat from pan, and return duck to cook with backside down. Add ½ cup water to pan, if needed to keep roast from sticking to bottom of pan. Continue roasting until duck is tender and skin is crisp, about 30 minutes. Juice should run clear, not pink when meat is pierced with a fork.

Transfer duck to a platter and allow it to set for 15 minutes. Slice meat from bones and keep warm. Remove stuffing from duck cavity and place on an ovenproof dish to keep warm while you make the gravy.

SERVES 4

GRAVY

1 cup drippings from roasting pan
Dash of salt and black pepper
3 tablespoons flour
1 cup chicken stock

Measure 1 cup drippings from pan; skim off fat. Return drippings to roasting pan; add salt, pepper, and flour to drippings; brown flour.

Add chicken stock and stir until gravy thickens. Pour into a gravy bowl and serve with duck.

MAKES ABOUT 2 CUPS

ROAST GOOSE
Sült Liba

Goose is notorious for the amount of fat rendered during cooking time. The fat is under the skin; the meat itself is lean. For this reason, the goose should be stuffed because the stuffing does not absorb the fat. Follow these directions for a moist, but relatively fat-free goose.

1 (9-to 12-pound) goose
Salt
Pepper
Stuffing (page 106)
Giblet gravy (page 102)

Preheat the oven to 325 degrees.

Remove the neck and giblets; rinse and reserve for gravy. Remove and discard any lumps of fat in the neck and breast cavities. Pull out any quills in the skin. Small pliers work well for this. Prick the skin all over with a sharp needle being careful not to puncture the meat.

Sprinkle the goose with salt and pepper to taste. Loosely pack stuffing into neck and breast cavities and close both openings by sewing or using thin skewers.

Place the goose, breast side down, in a roasting pan and cook for 1½ hours; remove the goose from the oven and spoon out most of the fat in the pan.

Return the goose, breast side up, to the pan and cook 1 to 1½ hours or until the drumstick feels soft when pressed.

For extra-crispy skin, raise oven temperature to 400 degrees and roast the goose for 15 more minutes. Remove the goose from the roasting pan and let stand for 15 minutes.

Spoon fat from roasting pan, saving all juice and brown bits. Place pan on stove burner at medium; add ½ cup water. Simmer the mixture while scraping the bottom of the pan with a wooden spoon. Season with salt and pepper to taste and add to giblet gravy.

SERVES 8

GIBLET GRAVY FOR TURKEY, DUCK, OR GOOSE

Aprolék Mártás Pulyka, Kacsa, vagy Libának

For gravy with greater depth of flavor, giblets are simmered with the vegetables.

4 cups chicken stock
Giblets from turkey
1 onion, quartered
½ cup chopped celery
1 cup chopped carrots
5 sprigs Italian parsley
¾ cup water
5 tablespoons flour
Paprika
Salt
Pepper

To chicken stock, add giblets, onion, celery, carrots, and parsley. Partially cover and simmer slowly for 1 to 1½ hours, or until giblets are tender.

Strain stock through a sieve and discard vegetables. Chop giblets into small pieces. Return chopped organs to the stock.

While bringing stock to a low boil, mix together the water and flour. Pour the mixture into gently boiling stock, stirring constantly while stock thickens.

Pour fat off roasting pan and discard. With heat of two stovetop burners under the roasting pan, scrape together any brown bits or juices from the bottom of the pan. Add ¼ to ½ cup water to help loosen cooked bits. Pour in thickened gravy and mix with juices from roast. Add paprika, salt, and pepper to taste.

Pour into a gravy boat and serve with your roast bird.

MAKES ABOUT 4 CUPS GRAVY

GIZZARDS AND RICE
Zuza és Rizs

Gizzards are sold in bulk at most supermarkets. Tough to chew if not cooked properly, gizzards become a delicacy when cooked to tenderness. Before cooking, cut away and discard the tough membrane connecting the lobes.

1 pound chicken gizzards
3 cups chicken stock (see page 57)
1 cup sliced onion
1 cup chopped celery
1 cup sliced carrots
½ cup chopped tomato
1½ cups uncooked rice
1 tablespoon chopped fresh Italian parsley

Place gizzards and stock in a 3-quart saucepan and bring to a boil. Skim foam from top. Add onion, lower heat; cover and cook until giblets are tender, 1 to 1½ hours.

Remove gizzards from the broth with a slotted spoon and cut into ¼-inch slices. Return gizzards to pan; add celery, carrots, tomato, and rice. Bring to a boil, lower heat, cover and cook 20 minutes, or until liquid is absorbed. Stir in parsley.

Serves 6 to 8

OLD-FASHIONED ROAST TURKEY
Sült Pulyka

Prepare bread stuffing (see page 106) to fill the bird's cavity or use your choice of stuffing. Allow about ½ cup stuffing per pound of turkey. If you purchased a frozen turkey, be sure it is completely thawed. It takes 3 days to thaw a 15-pound turkey ***in the refrigerator***.

1 (12-to 14-pound) turkey
2 to 3 teaspoons salt
½ teaspoon pepper
¼ pound butter, melted
1 teaspoon lemon juice

Preheat oven to 325 degrees.

Remove giblet bag from turkey cavity; reserve the heart, liver, giblet, and neck for the gravy. Rinse turkey inside and outside with cold water, and pat dry with paper towels. Rub salt and pepper into cavity.

Loosely pack stuffing into neck and breast cavity and skewer or truss both ends to hold stuffing in place. Place any excess stuffing in a greased baking dish and put into the oven during last hour of turkey's cooking time.

Tie drumsticks together with kitchen twine, and tuck wings under bird to keep tips from burning.

Spray a shallow roasting pan with vegetable oil. Place turkey, breast-side up into the pan. Combine butter and lemon juice, and brush over turkey.

Place the turkey on a rack in the bottom third of the oven. Roast, uncovered, until the meat thermometer placed in one of the thighs reaches 175 degrees. A turkey requires 20 minutes per pound of roasting time. The stuffing must reach 165 degrees for safe eating. Continue to baste with the melted butter every half hour. When the turkey is done, let it rest at room temperature for 20 minutes before carving.

SERVES 8 TO 10

POULTRY STUFFING
Csirke Töltelék

This recipe makes enough bread dressing to stuff a 4- to 5-pound chicken, duck, or goose. To stuff a turkey, double the ingredients. For an interesting texture, add 1 cup chopped water chestnuts.

1 chicken bouillon cube
1 cup hot water
8 slices day-old white bread
2 tablespoons vegetable oil
½ cup chopped onion
½ cup chopped celery
1 cup sliced fresh mushrooms
2 eggs, beaten
½ teaspoon salt
¼ teaspoon pepper
½ cup chopped fresh parsley
Liver from poultry to be roasted, chopped fine

Dissolve bouillon cube in water. In a large bowl, tear bread into roughly 1-inch pieces. Sprinkle just enough bouillon over bread to barely moisten. Stir a few times to catch any dry pieces that may need moistening.

Heat oil in a medium skillet; sauté onion, celery, and mushrooms until vegetables are just turning soft (5 to 8 minutes).

Stir sautéed vegetables, eggs, salt, pepper, parsley, and liver into bread pieces; stir only until all ingredients are evenly distributed. Dressing should be light and fluffy.

Fill cavity of fowl and roast according to recipe directions.

MAKES 3 TO 4 CUPS STUFFING

TURKEY DRUMSTICKS PAPRIKA
Paprikás Pulyka Láb

2 tablespoons vegetable oil
1 cup chopped onion
½ pound fresh mushrooms, cleaned and sliced
4 small or 2 large turkey legs (turkey legs are sold in packages)
1½ teaspoons garlic salt
2 teaspoons paprika
¼ teaspoon black pepper
1 cup water
1 chicken bouillon cube
2 tablespoons flour, optional

Heat 1 tablespoon oil in a large skillet or a Dutch oven. Sauté onion and mushrooms on medium heat for 5 minutes. Remove vegetables with a slotted spoon and set aside.

Add remaining 1 tablespoon oil to skillet and heat. Place turkey legs into skillet. Season with garlic salt, paprika, and pepper. Braise legs, uncovered, on medium heat, until slightly browned. While legs are browning, heat water and dissolve bouillon cube. Return onion and mushrooms to skillet; add dissolved bouillon.

Cover, bring to a boil; reduce heat to low-medium and simmer about 1 hour, or until turkey is tender.

Remove turkey legs from the skillet; cut meat from the bones and dice into bite-size pieces. Before returning diced turkey to skillet, thicken the sauce.

TO THICKEN SAUCE

Mix the flour into ½ cup water. Add to simmering liquid, stirring until sauce thickens. If sauce is pale in color, add more paprika. Adjust other seasonings.

Return meat to the sauce. Serve over rice or wide noodles.

SERVES 4

Meats

STUFFED CABBAGE
Töltött Káposzta

This classic recipe of meat, rice, and vegetables is an example of a dish that has been adapted by many cultures over hundreds of years. Food historians believe that the original recipe was perfected by the ancient Turks who incorporated ground lamb and rice with currants and pine nuts, then wrapped the mixture in cabbage leaves. Through the centuries, variations of this recipe evolved until each Eastern and Central European country claimed its own version. When these Europeans migrated to the New World in the late nineteenth century, they brought their favorite stuffed cabbage recipes with them. Here is a Hungarian version.

1 large head cabbage
¾ pound ground beef
¾ pound ground pork
1 cup uncooked long-grain rice
1 cup chopped onion
1 teaspoon salt (plus another pinch or two)
½ teaspoon black pepper
1 can (28 ounces) sauerkraut, drained
1 can (16 ounces) tomato juice
2 smoked pork hocks, *or* 1 pound smoked sausage (*kolbász*), cut into serving pieces

Roux, Optional

3 tablespoons solid vegetable shortening
3 tablespoons flour
1 cup cold water
1 cup broth from cooking pot
1 cup sour cream

To prepare cabbage leaves, remove core from the center with a sharp knife. Place the cabbage head in a large saucepan and add water to cover. Bring to a boil; cover pot and boil 5 to 8 minutes. Don't allow leaves to become too soft. Remove cabbage and place in a colander to drain. Discard all but 4 cups cooking liquid. Separate cabbage leaves. With a paring knife, thin down the thick spine of each leaf so that the leaf curls around the meat mixture easily. Chop the small leaves near the core and reserve.

While the cabbage is cooking, mix the meat, rice, onion, 1 teaspoon salt, and pepper thoroughly. Place about 2 tablespoons of meat mixture on the wide end of each leaf. Roll up, tucking in the sides. With the seam side down, place in a heavy 10-quart pot. Hint: If you have more meat than leaves, form mixture into meatballs and add to pot.

Place the larger rolls on the bottom of the pot and build 3 or 4 layers. Cover with chopped cabbage leaves and sauerkraut. Add reserved liquid; pour tomato juice over all, distributing evenly. Place smoked meat on top.

Cover; cook on medium high for 15 minutes. Reduce heat to low and simmer 1½ hours.

The stuffed cabbage can be served at this point, or go one step further to make a roux-based sauce.

To prepare roux: In a medium skillet melt the shortening. Add the flour; blend and cook over low heat, stirring constantly until mixture turns light brown. Turn off heat; add the cold water and whisk until smooth. Whisk the broth into the flour. (It may be necessary to remove a layer of rolls to reach the broth). Pour roux into the pot and stir until roux and broth are blended. Bring to a gentle boil and cook 10 minutes; broth will thicken into a rich sauce.

Remove 1 cup sauce, cool a few minutes and mix with the sour cream. Pour sour cream mixture over cabbage rolls. Make sure the sour cream sauce descends below the top layer of rolls. Cover and simmer 10 minutes.

MAKES 15 TO 18 ROLLS

Stuffed Cabbage.

NEW WORLD STUFFED CABBAGE

1 large head cabbage
1 can (16 ounces) sauerkraut
2 tablespoons vegetable oil
½ cup finely chopped onion
2 cloves garlic, minced
¼ cup flour
1 tablespoon Hungarian paprika
1 can (16 ounces) tomatoes, crushed
2 cups beef broth
½ cup long-grain rice, uncooked
1 pound ground turkey
2 tablespoons chopped fresh Italian parsley
1 teaspoon salt
½ teaspoon black pepper
1 egg, beaten

Prepare cabbage as on page 111.

Heat oven to 350 degrees

Spoon half the sauerkraut into the bottom of a Dutch oven; set aside. In a medium saucepan heat oil; sauté onion and garlic until tender. Remove half to a bowl to cool. To the remaining onion mixture add flour and paprika. Cook and stir 1 to 2 minutes. Stir in tomatoes and broth; bring to a boil. Remove from heat and set aside. To cooled onion mixture, add rice, turkey, parsley, salt, pepper, and egg; mix well. Place about 2 tablespoons of the mixture on each cabbage leaf. Roll up and tuck in sides. Place rolls, seam side down, on sauerkraut in Dutch oven. Cover with remaining sauerkraut. Pour tomato mixture over all, adding water to cover if necessary. Cover and bake about 2 hours.

MAKES ABOUT 12 CABBAGE ROLLS

For a Transylvanian flavor, wrap the meat mixture in grape leaves and garnish with Cherry Sauce (page 40).

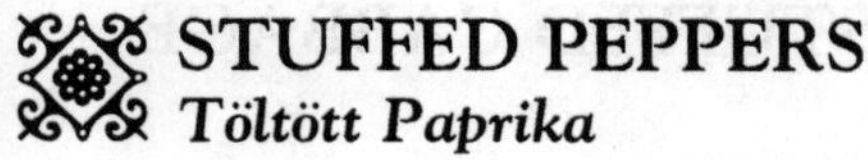

STUFFED PEPPERS
Töltött Paprika

8 medium green peppers
½ pound lean ground beef
½ pound lean ground pork
½ cup minced onion
¾ cup uncooked rice
1 teaspoon salt
½ teaspoon pepper
1½ teaspoons sugar
3 cups tomato juice
1 cup sour cream

Wash peppers, cut off tops, and remove seeds.

Mix together beef, pork, onion, rice, salt, and pepper. Fill green peppers about ⅔ full with meat mixture. Place peppers into a deep pot. Mix sugar into tomato juice and pour juice over peppers. If peppers aren't covered, add more juice.

Simmer for about an hour or until rice and meat are cooked.

In a small bowl, slightly cool (about 5 minutes) 1 cup of juice from the cooking pot; mix in sour cream. Add mixture to the pot and stir.

SERVES 4 TO 6

HOMEMADE HUNGARIAN SAUSAGE
Magyar Kolbász

Today, few Hungarian-Americans go to the trouble of butchering pigs for fresh cuts of pork, but many continue the tradition of making their own sausages. Casings can usually be purchased in European butcher shops.

4 pounds coarsely-ground pork (not too lean or sausage will be dry)
4 cloves garlic, minced
2 tablespoons salt
1½ teaspoons black pepper
1 tablespoon paprika
3 yards sausage casing

Combine meat, garlic, salt, pepper, and paprika; mix thoroughly. Wash casing and fill with meat mixture using a sausage stuffing machine. You will have to borrow this from an old-timer or ask your friendly neighborhood butcher for help. Tie the ends with heavy string.

If sausage is not to be cooked immediately, it needs to be refrigerated, frozen, or smoked. Refrigerate no longer than 4 days; freeze no longer than 3 months.

To bake the sausage, preheat the oven to 350 degrees. Bake in a greased 9 × 13-inch baking pan, until sausage turns golden brown, about 45 minutes.

To smoke the sausage, place it in a smoker (unless you have a smokehouse) for 4 hours, them store the sausage in a cool place.

To cook the sausage stove-top, place 3 or 4 links in a heavy skillet. Cover with ½ inch water. Cover skillet, bring to a gentle boil, turn heat to low and simmer until sausage begins to turn reddish. Turn sausage over and add ½ cup water. Cover and continue cooking. When both sides are reddish-brown, remove cover and continue cooking on low heat until all the water has cooked away. Total cooking time is 35 to 45 minutes.

SERVES 6 TO 8

GOULASH AND DUMPLINGS
Gulyás Galuskával

Goulash is the ancestor of all stews. Its origin is traced to the ninth century when Magyar shepherds living on the plains made this hearty meal in large kettles over an open fire. There are many variations of this popular dish; two are presented here.

4 slices bacon, diced
1½ cups chopped onions
2 pounds beef, cut into 1½-inch chunks
1 tablespoon Hungarian paprika
1½ teaspoons salt
¼ teaspoon freshly ground pepper
¼ teaspoon marjoram
2 cups beef broth
¾ cup dry red wine
½ cup water
½ cup flour
Dumplings (page 80)

Place the bacon in a 6- to 8- quart pot and cook slowly until lightly browned. Remove bacon with slotted spoon and set aside.

Add onions to bacon fat and cook over medium heat until soft. Remove onions with slotted spoon, and set aside.

Add beef to bacon fat and brown slowly on all sides. When browned, add paprika, salt, pepper, and marjoram.

Stir in reserved bacon/onion mixture. Pour in meat broth and wine. Bring to a boil. Reduce heat, cover pot, and simmer on low heat 1½ hours, or until meat is tender when pierced with a fork. Combine water and flour, and stir into pot; simmer 5 to 8 minutes, or until broth thickens into a gravy.

Serve with dumplings. Note: Spoon 3 to 4 tablespoons gravy over dumplings just before serving.

SERVES 6 TO 8

NEW WORLD GOULASH

2 tablespoons vegetable oil
1 cup chopped onion
2 pounds chuck beef, cut into 1½-inch cubes
1 teaspoon paprika
2 teaspoons salt
¼ teaspoon black pepper
1 fresh tomato, diced
1 green pepper, seeded and chopped
2 cups water
2 cups sliced carrots
1 cup sliced celery
3 large white rose potatoes, diced

Heat oil; sauté onions until soft. Add beef, paprika, salt, and black pepper. Mix seasonings with meat; brown meat on all sides.

Add tomato, green pepper, and water. Bring to a boil; reduce heat, cover and cook slowly for 1½ hours. Add carrots, celery and potatoes. Cover and cook slowly for another ½ hour, or until the vegetables are tender.

Serve as a main dish with thick slices of rye bread.

SERVES 6

Hungarian Swiss Steak.

HUNGARIAN SWISS STEAK
Magyaros Svájci Marhaszelet

The rich, sour cream gravy in this dish pairs well with dumplings, wide noodles, or rice.

2½ pounds round steak
1 teaspoon salt
½ teaspoon pepper
1½ teaspoons paprika
3 tablespoons butter
3 tablespoons flour
1 cup chopped onion
½ cup chopped green pepper
½ cup diced tomatoes (fresh or canned)
8 ounces fresh mushrooms, sliced
1 cup water
½ cup sour cream

Cut steak into serving portions. Pound each piece with a tenderizer mallet. Combine salt, pepper, paprika, and flour in a shallow plate. Dredge both sides of steak pieces with the flour mixture.

In a large heavy skillet, melt butter and brown both sides of meat pieces in hot butter until light brown. Remove meat; using the same skillet add onions, green pepper, tomatoes, and mushrooms. Sauté vegetables for 5 minutes. Return meat to pan. Add water; cover and simmer on low heat for 1½ hours, or until meat is tender.

Remove meat to a warm serving plate. Raise heat to medium for gentle boil. Mix sour cream with 1 cup of sauce from skillet; add this mixture to the skillet, stirring constantly until the gravy thickens. Pour gravy over the meat and serve.

SERVES 4 TO 6

NEW WORLD VERSION

Use 2 tablespoons vegetable oil instead of butter. Reduce sour cream to ¼ cup.

LAYERED PORK WITH RICE
Rakott Disznóhus Rizsával

A busy cook must have devised this variation of stuffed cabbage. It contains all the ingredients of that classic dish, but eliminates the need to roll the meat mixture into parboiled cabbage leaves. The rich flavor remains, but preparation time is reduced. This dish may also be baked as a casserole in a 350-degree oven, but I prefer cooking it on top of the stove because the end result tastes more moist.

1 tablespoon vegetable oil
1 cup chopped onion
1½ pounds lean ground pork
1 teaspoon salt
1 teaspoon pepper
1 cup uncooked rice
1 can (27 ounces) sauerkraut, drained
1½ cups sour cream
2 cups chopped cabbage
2 cups tomato juice

Heat oil in a large, heavy skillet; sauté onions until soft.

Place meat in a large bowl; season with salt and pepper. Mix in rice; add sautéed onions and mix well.

In the same skillet used for cooking onions, layer meat mixture, sauerkraut, and sour cream, in that order, one-third at a time. Spread chopped cabbage over the last layer of sour cream. Pour tomato juice over all. Cover tightly and bring to a boil. Reduce heat to low and cook 1 hour, or until rice is tender.

SERVES 6

PORK STEW WITH SAUERKRAUT
Székely Gulyás

This recipe is the result of improvisation by a man named Székely, who arrived at a restaurant in Hungary too late to choose from the menu. He asked the owner to serve the leftover sauerkraut and some cooked pork on the same plate. The story has it that the poet Petöfi Sándor was within hearing distance and the following day asked the owner for Székely's *guylás*, the same mixture Mr. Székely had been served the day before. This time the cook added sour cream and since that day this dish has become a classic.

George Lang's account in *The Cuisine of Hungary*

2½ pounds diced pork butt
3 tablespoons vegetable oil
2 cups chopped onion
2 cloves garlic, crushed
1 teaspoon salt
½ teaspoon black pepper
2 teaspoons paprika
2 cans (15 ounces each) sauerkraut, drained
½ cup sour cream

Brown the pork in hot oil; keep heat at medium high while browning the meat. Add the onions, garlic, salt, pepper, and paprika. Lower heat, cover and simmer until the meat is tender, 45 to 60 minutes. Add sauerkraut and mix in gently. Stir in sour cream just before serving.

Any dark fresh bread is a perfect match for this recipe.

SERVES 8

JELLIED PIGS' FEET
Kocsonya

For many Hungarian families, jellied pigs' feet is a traditional New Year's Day food. This must be made a day or two before eating because the broth needs 24 hours to jell in the refrigerator. Rye bread, cut into thick slices, is just the right texture of bread to eat with this dish.

6 pigs' feet (almost all grocery stores carry them)
4 quarts water
2 teaspoons paprika
2 tablespoons salt
1 teaspoon pepper
1 onion, whole
4 cloves garlic

If pig's feet are large, ask the butcher to cut them into halves. Place feet into a large pot with the water and bring to boiling point; remove foam that comes to the top. Add paprika, salt, pepper, onion, and garlic. Lower heat, cover, and simmer for 2 to 2½ hours. Divide pigs' feet and place skin side up into 6 soup bowls. Pour strained broth over the feet. Sprinkle each dish with paprika. Cool slightly and refrigerate overnight.

SERVES 6

Variation:

Chop the onion; add diced potatoes and carrots during last half hour of cooking and eat as a hot stew.

EASY HUNGARIAN PORK CHOP CASSEROLE
Könnyű Rakott Disznohus

4 tablespoons butter
2 cloves garlic, minced
5 medium red rose potatoes, sliced thin
4 cups coarsely chopped cabbage
4 to 6 pork chops
Salt
Pepper
Paprika

Heat oven to 400 degrees.

In a 9 × 13-inch baking dish, melt butter and stir in garlic, potato slices, and cabbage. Place pork chops on top. Season chops with salt, pepper, and paprika.

Bake 50 to 60 minutes. Chops will be nicely browned.

SERVES 4 TO 6

NEW WORLD PORK CHOP CASSEROLE

1 package (5½ ounces) potatoes au gratin
4 cups coarsely chopped cabbage
4 pork chops, trimmed of fat
Garlic salt
Pepper
Paprika

Preheat oven to 400 degrees.

Prepare potatoes according to directions, except increase water to 2½ cups. Stir the cabbage into the potatoes; place pork chops on top. Season chops with garlic salt, pepper, and paprika. Bake 50 to 60 minutes until chops are brown.

SERVES 4

GLAZED BAKED HAM
Sütött Sonka

This glaze can be used with a lamb or pork roast as well.

1 cooked half ham, butt or shank end, 5 to 7 pounds
1 tablespoon whole cloves, optional

Glaze

¾ cup apricot jam
¼ cup yellow or brown mustard
¼ teaspoon ground cloves

Preheat oven to 350 degrees.

Position rack in the lower third of the oven. Place ham in a shallow roasting pan and put into oven. Bake 10 to 12 minutes per pound. Bake until meat thermometer inserted into the thickest part of the ham reads 140 degrees.

To make glaze, combine jam, mustard, and ground cloves in a small saucepan and simmer 5 minutes. Remove ham 30 minutes before it is done, score the top with a sharp knife to make a grid pattern. Insert whole cloves at this point, if desired; brush on glaze. Return ham to the oven to finish baking.

Serves 10 to 12

ROASTED LEG OF LAMB
Sült Bárány Comb

Roasted to medium-rare and simply seasoned, leg of lamb has an almost buttery flavor that melts in the mouth. For best results, position the oven rack in the lower third of the oven.

1 leg of lamb, 5 to 6 pounds, bone in
2 cloves garlic, cut into 10 slivers
2 tablespoons olive oil
2 teaspoons garlic salt
1 teaspoon coarsely ground black pepper
1 onion, quartered
8 peeled carrots
8 unpeeled red rose potatoes
½ cup water
Glaze, optional (see page 128)

Preheat oven to 450 degrees.

With a sharp knife, remove most of the layer of fat from leg; discard. Leave just enough fat to keep the meat moist. Cut 10 deep slits in the roast and insert the garlic slivers.

Rub olive oil over the surface of the roast and season with garlic salt and pepper. Place the roast with meatier side up in a large roasting pan. Arrange onion, carrots, and potatoes around the meat. Add water.

Place roasting pan, without cover, into the oven. Immediately reduce heat to 350 degrees. Roast until meat thermometer registers 135 to 145 degrees for medium rare (about 1½ hours). If glazing roast, brush over surface 20 minutes before end of cooking time.

Transfer lamb to a serving platter and let stand 10 minutes before carving. Place cooked vegetables on another serving platter.

Pour off fat from cooking juices. Simmer liquid until slightly thickened. Serve the juice with carved lamb and vegetables.

SERVES 8 TO 10

GLAZE FOR LAMB ROAST
Cukrász Máz

This fruit-based glaze enhances the flavor of lamb.

½ cup apricot preserves
¼ cup sherry
½ teaspoon freshly grated ginger
1 teaspoon lemon juice
1 teaspoon prepared mustard

Heat preserves and sherry. Remove from heat; stir in ginger, lemon, and mustard. Brush on roast during the last 20 minutes of cooking time to avoid the sugar in preserves from burning before the meat is cooked.

ENOUGH FOR A 4-TO 5-POUND ROAST.

LAMB SHANKS
Bárány Lábszár

This is a hearty dish that tastes especially good on a cold night.

2 cloves garlic, minced
4 lamb shanks
Salt
Pepper
1 tablespoon vegetable oil
8 carrots, cut in 2-inch pieces
1 cup chopped onion
½ pound fresh mushrooms, sliced
½ cup sliced celery
4 potatoes, cut into quarters
½ cup water

Spread garlic over each shank. Season to taste with salt and pepper.

Heat oil in a Dutch oven; brown shanks on all sides. Add carrots, onion, mushrooms, celery, potatoes, and water. Cover and simmer 1½ hours, or until meat is tender.

SERVES 4

STUFFED BREAST OF VEAL
Töltött Borju

Breast of veal lends itself well to this recipe because it comes with its own pocket, a membrane layer for holding the stuffing and keeping it intact.

4 to 5 pounds breast of veal
1½ to 2 teaspoons salt
Paprika
Black pepper
4 slices bacon

STUFFING
6 slices white bread, slightly dried (2-to 3-day-old bread)
1 to 1½ cups water
¼ pound margarine
1 cup finely chopped onion
1 cup finely chopped celery
2 eggs, beaten
3 tablespoons minced fresh Italian parsley
1 teaspoon salt
¼ teaspoon black pepper

Preheat oven to 350 degrees.

Wash veal; sprinkle with salt and set aside while preparing the stuffing.

To make the stuffing, soak bread in water (about 5 minutes). Meanwhile, melt margarine; sauté onion and celery until vegetables are soft.

Press water out of the bread with hands and tear into small pieces. Place pieces into a large bowl; mix in eggs. Add onion, celery, parsley, salt, and pepper; mix together gently.

Stuff veal pocket and truss edges together by sewing or using thin skewers. Place veal in a greased roasting pan; lightly sprinkle veal with paprika, salt, and pepper. Place bacon on top; add 1 cup water to pan; cover and roast for about 2 hours.

Remove cover and the bacon strips. Roast meat 15 minutes longer to brown the meat, basting occasionally. Add more water if needed.

SERVES 4 TO 6

VEAL PAPRIKA
Borju Paprikás

4 slices bacon
1 cup chopped onion
½ cup chopped green pepper
½ cup flour
1 teaspoon salt
¼ teaspoon black pepper
2 teaspoons paprika
2 pounds veal stew meat, cubed
½ cup water

SAUCE
1 tablespoon shortening
1 tablespoon flour
1 teaspoon paprika
½ cup milk
1 cup sour cream, room temperature

Cook bacon in a deep 12-inch skillet, or Dutch oven until crisp. Remove bacon, chop into ¼-inch pieces and set aside. Sauté onion and green pepper in bacon grease until onion is lightly browned. With a slotted spoon, remove onion and green pepper from skillet and set aside.

Combine flour, salt, pepper, and paprika in a plastic bag. Place veal cubes into bag and shake until meat is coated with flour mixture.

Heat the bacon grease left in the skillet to medium high and brown meat on all sides.

Return bacon, onion, and green pepper to the skillet. Add water; cover and simmer 45 minutes, or until veal is tender. Stir occasionally and add water as needed.

When veal is cooked, prepare the sauce. In a small saucepan, melt shortening. Blend in flour and paprika; stir until smooth. Cook on medium heat until mixture bubbles, stirring constantly.

Gradually stir in the milk; return gentle boil, stirring constantly. Cook 1 minute; remove from heat. Beat with a whisk or fork; add sour cream in small amounts. Mix well.

Pour sauce into the veal mixture, stirring constantly. Continue cooking mixture 3 minutes. Serve with dumplings (see page 80)

SERVES 6

NEW WORLD VEAL PAPRIKA

3 tablespoons vegetable shortening
1 cup chopped onion
1½ pounds veal stew meat, cubed
2 teaspoons salt
¼ teaspoon black pepper
2 teaspoons paprika
½ cup chopped tomato
½ cup water
4 medium potatoes, peeled and diced

Heat shortening; add onions and simmer on low heat until transparent. Add veal, sprinkle with salt, pepper, and paprika. Stir in tomatoes and water. Cover and simmer for ½ hour. Add potatoes and simmer for 15 more minutes, or until potatoes are tender.

Variation:

Add sliced carrots and/or cabbage chunks along with potatoes.

SERVES 4

HOT DOG STEW
Virslipaprikás

This is a "busy day" stew. Easy to prepare, it provides a main dish in minutes. If you prefer, you may use turkey, chicken, or low-fat hot dogs.

1 tablespoon vegetable oil
1 medium-size onion, sliced
1 green pepper, sliced lengthwise
8 hot dogs, cut into 1-inch pieces
3 cans tomato sauce (8 ounces each)
½ cup water
½ teaspoon paprika

Heat oil in a 4-quart saucepan. Sauté onion and green pepper for 3 minutes. Add hot dogs; simmer with onions and green pepper for 5 minutes. Stir in tomato sauce, water, and paprika. Bring to a boil; reduce heat to low; cover and simmer for 5 minutes.

Variations:

Add fresh mushrooms and sauté with onions and green pepper.

Add canned mushrooms, including liquid. Omit water from recipe.

Add diced potatoes when adding hot dogs. This will lengthen cooking time, but you will have a meal-in-one dish.

SERVES 4

VEGETABLES

Mark Twain once said,
"Training is everything.
The peach was once a bitter almond;
cauliflower is nothing
but cabbage with a college education."

BAKED CAULIFLOWER WITH EGGS
Sült Karfiol Tojással

Sour cream sauce lifts cauliflower to gourmet status. Add hard-boiled eggs and you have a dish that takes center stage.

1 large head cauliflower, trimmed of blemishes, leaves, and woody base
½ teaspoon salt
1 cup water
¼ cup bread crumbs
½ cup grated Parmesan cheese
2 eggs
2 cups sour cream
4 hard-boiled eggs, peeled and sliced

Preheat oven to 350 degrees; lightly grease a 1½-quart casserole.

Rinse cauliflower, break into florets; cover and cook in lightly salted water over high heat 5 minutes. Cauliflower should be firm, not limp. Drain cauliflower and set aside.

Mix bread crumbs and Parmesan cheese; set aside.

In a medium bowl, beat raw eggs; blend in sour cream. Set sauce aside.

Arrange half of cauliflower and boiled eggs on the bottom of casserole. Spoon half of sauce over cauliflower and eggs. Distribute second half of cauliflower and eggs over this first layer. Pour remaining sauce over all. Sprinkle bread crumb mixture over top. Bake 25 to 30 minutes, or until top is lightly browned.

SERVES 6 TO 8

NEW WORLD BAKED CAULIFLOWER WITH EGGS

1 medium head cauliflower, trimmed of leaves and stem
½ teaspoon salt
½ cup water
1 egg
1 cup low-fat sour cream
2 hard-boiled eggs, peeled and sliced

Preheat oven to 350 degrees; grease bottom of a 1½-quart casserole dish with vegetable spray.

Rinse cauliflower and break into florets; cover and cook in salted water over high heat 5 minutes. Cauliflower should be firm. Drain cauliflower and set aside.

In a medium bowl, combine raw egg and sour cream; set aside.

Arrange cauliflower and boiled eggs on the bottom of casserole. Spoon the sauce over cauliflower and eggs. Bake 25 to 30 minutes, or until top is lightly browned.

SERVES 4 TO 6

SWEET AND SOUR CABBAGE
Édes és Savanyu Káposzta

A garden-fresh staple, cabbage was prepared in many forms, from soup to slaw. We continue to enjoy this versatile vegetable. Here is a sweet and sour cabbage that makes an excellent side dish to any meat entrée.

4 slices bacon
1 medium head cabbage, chopped
1 large onion, sliced
1 teaspoon paprika
2 tablespoons sugar
1 teaspoon salt
¼ cup vinegar
½ cup tomato juice
½ cup water
1 apple, grated
¼ teaspoon black pepper

In a 4-quart nonaluminum pan, fry bacon until crisp, remove from pan and set aside. Discard all but 2 tablespoons bacon fat; sauté cabbage and onion in fat while stirring mixture for about 5 minutes. Add paprika, sugar, salt, vinegar, tomato juice, water, apple, and pepper. Cover and cook on low heat for about 15 minutes, until cabbage is tender. Stir occasionally. Dice bacon and add to cabbage near the end of cooking time.

SERVES 4 TO 6

LENTILS WITH VEGETABLES
Lencse Zöldséggel

1 tablespoon vegetable oil
1 onion, chopped
2 carrots, chopped
2 stalks celery, chopped
2 cups vegetable broth
1 cup dry lentils, washed (this will double in volume when cooked)
¼ teaspoon black pepper
1 teaspoon vinegar

Heat oil in a 4-quart saucepan. Sauté onion, carrots, and celery for 5 minutes.

Add broth, lentils, and black pepper. Bring to a boil; reduce heat to low. Cover and simmer 35 to 40 minutes, or until lentils are tender. Add vinegar during last 5 minutes of cooking.

SERVES 6

MUSHROOM PAPRIKA
Paprikás Gomba

2 tablespoons vegetable oil
1 cup chopped onion
1 teaspoon salt
¼ teaspoon black pepper
1 tablespoon paprika
1 pound mushrooms, washed, cut in halves
1 cup chicken or beef broth
1 tablespoon flour

Heat oil in a 10-inch skillet. Add onions and cook until soft. Add salt, pepper, paprika, mushrooms and broth. Mix well and cook until mushrooms are tender, 10 to 15 minutes. Sprinkle flour over mushrooms, stir and cook about 3 minutes, or until sauce is thickened.

SERVES 4

DILLED SQUASH WITH SOUR CREAM
Tejfeles Tök Főzelék

This is an all-seasons dish—served cool in the spring and summer, warm in the fall and winter. With the addition of more stock, it becomes a uniquely flavored creamy soup.

3 pounds crookneck or summer squash
1 tablespoon salt
2 tablespoons butter
2 tablespoons flour
1 cup grated onion
3 tablespoons minced fresh dill, or 1 tablespoon dry dill
1 cup vegetable or chicken stock
1 to 2 tablespoons white vinegar
1 teaspoon sugar
½ cup sour cream

Peel the squash, remove seeds, and cut into 2-inch chunks. Grate the squash using the grating blade of your food processor. If you don't have a processor, use the largest holes of a four-sided, handheld grater. Place squash into a bowl, sprinkle with salt, cover, and let stand 45 to 60 minutes.

Meanwhile, in a 3-quart saucepan, melt butter and mix in flour. Cook on low heat, stirring constantly with a wooden spoon, until flour turns golden. Add onion. When onion becomes light brown, add the dill and stir.

Stir stock into flour/onion mixture and cook on medium heat until stock thickens. Hint: stir with a whisk to prevent lumps from forming.

Squeeze moisture from grated squash and add squash to pot. Cook, uncovered, on medium heat for 15 minutes. Add vinegar and sugar, and cook 5 more minutes. Adjust sweetness or sourness to taste.

Lower heat and mix in sour cream. Serve warm, or chill and serve cold.

SERVES 4 TO 6

RICE AND VEGETABLES
Rizs és Zöldség

Easy to prepare, this recipe is an excellent accompaniment to any main dish. By adding cubes of tender veal, chicken, or pork while sautéing vegetables, it becomes a complete meal in itself. The beauty of this recipe is that, as in soup, you can add or subtract meat or vegetables to create your own masterpiece.

1 tablespoon vegetable oil
1 cup chopped onion
1 cup sliced celery
1 cup sliced carrots
1 cup uncooked rice
2 cups chicken or vegetable broth (see page 57)
1 tablespoon chopped fresh parsley

In a 3-quart saucepan, heat oil; sauté onion, celery, and carrots for 5 minutes. Add rice and broth; bring to a boil, reduce heat. Cover and cook on low heat 20 minutes. Turn off heat; stir in parsley.

SERVES 6

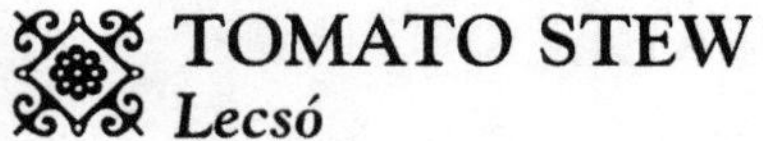

TOMATO STEW
Lecsó

This recipe is superb when made with garden-fresh tomatoes. If Hungarian peppers (long and pale green) are not available, substitute green bell peppers. This shines alone as a side dish, or, paired with Hungarian sausage, becomes an entrée. It is also delicious served over a scoop of mashed potatoes or cooked rice.

1 tablespoon vegetable or canola oil
¾ cup sliced onion
1 tablespoon Hungarian paprika
3 large, very ripe tomatoes, peeled and diced (if tomatoes are hard to peel, plunge into boiling water for a few seconds)
6 Hungarian peppers, seeded and cut into 1-inch strips
1 teaspoon sugar
1 teaspoon salt

Heat oil in a medium saucepan. Add onion and sauté over medium heat for 6 to 8 minutes. Stir in paprika. Reduce heat to low.

Stir in tomatoes, peppers, sugar, and salt.

Cover and cook over low heat until peppers are limp, 20 to 25 minutes.

SERVES 4

POTATOES PAPRIKA
Paprikás Krumpli

These potatoes are easy to make and go well with pork or ham.

4 slices bacon
1 onion, sliced
1 green pepper, cut into strips
5 cups potatoes, cut into ¼-inch slices
1½ teaspoon paprika
½ teaspoon salt
¼ teaspoon black pepper
½ cup water

In a 3-quart saucepan, fry bacon until crisp; remove bacon from pan and set aside. Into the bacon drippings add onion and green pepper; simmer about 5 minutes. Add potatoes and sprinkle with paprika, salt, and pepper; stir to distribute seasonings. Add water; cover, and cook until potatoes are tender, about 20 minutes. Crumble the bacon strips and mix into the potatoes.

SERVES 4 TO 5

NEW WORLD VERSION

Omit bacon. Sauté onion and pepper in 1 tablespoon vegetable oil.

HUNGARIAN SCALLOPED POTATOES WITH SAUSAGE

Rakott Krumpli Kolbásszal

¼ pound butter, melted
⅔ cup bread crumbs
4 cups sliced, cooked white rose or red-skinned potatoes
½ pound smoked Hungarian sausage, thinly sliced
6 hard-boiled eggs, sliced
Salt
Pepper
1 cup sour cream
¼ cup milk

Preheat oven to 350 degrees.

Place 4 tablespoons melted butter in the bottom of a 9 × 13-inch baking dish. Sprinkle 3 tablespoons bread crumbs over butter. Layer half of the potatoes, sausage, and egg slices in that order. Season each layer (except the sausage slices) with a sprinkling of salt and pepper to taste. Pour remainder of butter over all; spread bread crumbs to cover. Mix sour cream with milk and pour over the top.

Bake, uncovered, 30 minutes.

SERVES 6 TO 8

NEW WORLD SCALLOPED POTATOES

1 cup sour cream
1 egg, beaten
¼ cup milk
1 small onion, minced
½ teaspoon salt
¼ teaspoon black pepper
3 cups sliced, cooked white rose or red-skinned potatoes
4 hard-boiled eggs, sliced
Paprika

Preheat oven to 350 degrees.

Beat together sour cream, egg, milk, onion, salt, and pepper. Layer potatoes and eggs into 9 × 13-inch baking dish. Spoon some of the sour cream mixture over each layer, saving 3 tablespoons to pour over top. Sprinkle with paprika.

Bake, uncovered, for 30 minutes.

SERVES 6

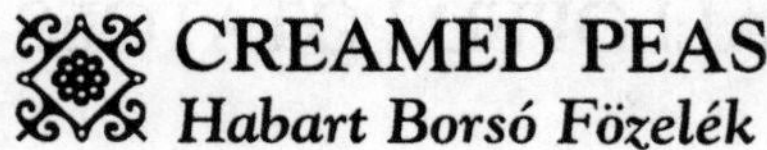

CREAMED PEAS
Habart Borsó Főzelék

1 tablespoon butter or margarine
1 tablespoon flour
¼ cup whole milk
1 can (15 ounces) peas; drain but reserve ½ cup liquid
½ teaspoon sugar

Melt the butter in a small saucepan. Add the flour and stir for 1 minute.

Slowly add the milk and stir on low heat. The sauce will thicken to the density of pudding in about 1 minute.

Add the reserved liquid from the canned peas and stir for 1 minute. The sauce will thin out a little, but should have the consistency of a light gravy.

Gently stir in the sugar and peas until well blended.

SERVES 4

HUNGARIAN CREAMED SPINACH
Magyaros Habart Spenot Főzelék

½ cup water, lightly salted
1 package (10 ounces) frozen chopped spinach
3 strips bacon
2 tablespoons flour
¾ cup whole milk
½ cup sour cream

Bring the water to a boil; place the frozen spinach into the water. Bring the water to a second boil, then reduce heat. Cover and simmer about 5 minutes, or until the spinach is tender. Using a sieve, drain the spinach into a bowl and reserve ¾ cup liquid.

Cook the bacon in the same pan until crisp. Remove the bacon and set aside. Discard all but 2 tablespoons of bacon drippings. Mix the flour into the bacon drippings. Add milk and reserved liquid from the spinach. Stir until well blended. If the sauce is lumpy, stir it with a whisk until smooth. Return spinach to the pan, add the sour cream and mix thoroughly. Crumble the bacon and use as a garnish.

NEW WORLD VERSION

Omit the bacon. Replace bacon drippings with 2 tablespoons margarine. Reduce sour cream to 2 tablespoons.

SERVES 4

Desserts

APPLE WALNUT PITA
Almás Diós Pite

Lacking the convenience of modern kitchen appliances, our grandmothers had to grind nuts in cast-iron, hand-cranked food grinders. Just putting it together, and later, cleaning the oil-laden or food-encrusted parts was a chore in itself. I thank the kitchen gods for food processors that simplify two steps in this recipe: grinding the walnuts and grating the apples. Note: Set out 7 eggs 1 hour before preparation time to reach room temperature

Dough

2 cups flour
2 tablespoons sugar
¼ teaspoon salt
½ pound cold, sweet butter, cut into chunks
1 egg
½ cup sour cream

Filling

6 eggs, yolks separated from whites
1 cup sugar
2 cups grated apples (about 3 medium), any variety
2 tablespoons bread crumbs
1 tablespoon flour
1 cup ground walnuts
Grated zest of 1 lemon

Topping

½ cup sugar
½ cup ground walnuts

Preheat the oven to 350 degrees.

First make the dough. Combine and mix flour, sugar, and salt. Use a pastry blender to cut butter into the flour mixture as you would in making pie crust. When the flour mixture and butter are evenly distributed, it will reach the texture of dry oatmeal. Add 1 egg and sour cream; mix until all dry particles are moist.

Divide the dough into two portions. Flour your pastry board and rolling pin; roll each half to a rectangle 9 × 13 inches in size.

To make the filling, beat 5 egg whites (reserve 1 egg white for topping) until stiff. Beat 6 egg yolks with sugar until thick. Mix in apples, bread crumbs, flour, walnuts, and zest. Fold in egg whites.

To make the topping, beat the reserved egg white with a fork and set aside. In a separate bowl, stir together the cup sugar and ground walnuts; set aside.

To assemble the pita, place one dough rectangle into a 9 × 13-inch baking pan. If sheet exceeds the size of the pan, bring any overlap up the sides. Spread filling over the dough. Place the second rectangle of dough over the filling. Brush dough with egg white that was set aside for the topping; spread sugar and nut mixture over top of cake. Bake 30 to 40 minutes, until golden brown. Cool completely before cutting.

MAKES 20 TO 24 SQUARES

WALNUT PITA
Diós Pite

Hungarian cooks have passed this recipe down through several generations. Egg whites give the walnuts an unexpected lightness.

FILLING

6 egg yolks
¾ cup sugar
1 cup ground walnuts
7 egg whites, beaten stiff

DOUGH

2 cups flour
2 tablespoons sugar
¼ teaspoon salt
½ pound cold butter
1 egg yolk (reserve white for filling)
½ cup sour cream
Powdered sugar

Preheat oven to 350 degrees.

To make the filling, beat egg yolks, sugar, and vanilla; mix in walnuts. Fold in egg whites.

To make the dough, mix flour, sugar, and salt. Cut butter into flour mixture until small pieces the size of peas form. Add egg yolk and sour cream; mix well.

Flour pastry board and rolling pin. Divide dough in half; roll each half into a sheet, large enough to fit into a 9 × 13-inch cake pan. Line the bottom of the pan with one sheet of rolled dough; spread filling over the bottom dough, then place the second sheet of dough on top of the filling.

Bake 30 to 40 minutes, or until golden brown. When cool, sprinkle with powdered sugar and cut into squares.

MAKES 20 TO 24 SQUARES

Plum Dumplings.

PLUM DUMPLINGS
Szilvás Gombóc

A dessert dish, these dumplings taste best immediately after cooking. If plums are out of season when the craving strikes, you may use canned plums or prune jam (*szilvás lekvár)* sold on the international shelf of your grocery store or in European markets.

Filling

12 Italian prune plums (small and oval in size), cut into halves, seeds removed, or 6 ripe purple plums, cut into quarters, pits removed

2 teaspoons sugar

Dough

3 potatoes, cooked and peeled
1½ cups flour
½ teaspoon salt
1 egg
1 tablespoon butter, at room temperature
3 to 4 quarts water

Coating

4 tablespoons unsalted butter
1 cup bread crumbs
3 tablespoons sugar

Sprinkle 2 teaspoons sugar over plum pieces; set aside.

Grate potatoes into a large bowl. Mix in flour, salt, egg, and butter until well blended and a smooth, soft ball of dough forms.

Pull out a ball of dough, about the size of a large walnut. Hold dough in the palm of one hand, and with the other hand, press it into a flat circle. (If the dough is sticky, dust hands with flour). Place a plum section in the center of the circle. Fold the dough over the fruit until plum is completely covered. Moisten edges of dough to seal the seams.

Bring water to a gentle boil. Drop several dumplings (about 8 at a time), into the boiling water and cook 15 minutes, stirring occasionally. Drain each portion in a colander. Continue until all dumplings are cooked.

While dumplings are cooking, prepare the coating. Melt the butter in a large, heavy skillet; add bread crumbs and 3 tablespoons sugar; stir over low heat 10 to 15 minutes, until breadcrumbs are a golden brown. Roll the barely wet dumplings in the crumbs until each is covered. Dumplings are now ready to be served.

Makes 24 dumplings

APRICOT SQUARES
Barack Sütemény

Sour cream gives this cake its rich, flaky crust. The apricot filling may be cooked from dry apricots (see page 173). Canned apricot butter also works well in this recipe and can be found in the international section of most grocery stores. Regular apricot jam or preserves are too thin and runny.

¼ pound butter, at room temperature
¾ cup sugar
3 egg yolks
2 cups flour
1 teaspoon baking powder
1 teaspoon baking soda
¼ teaspoon salt
1 teaspoon vanilla
1 cup plus 1 tablespoon sour cream
2 cans (12 ounces each) apricot filling, or 3 cups cooked filling

TOPPING

1 to 1½ cups ground walnuts
½ cup sugar

Preheat oven to 350 degrees. Lightly grease a 9 × 13-inch pan with solid shortening.

Cream butter and sugar well. Add yolks, one at a time, beating well after each egg. In another bowl sift flour, baking powder, baking soda, and salt; add to the butter mixture. Add vanilla and sour cream; blend well.

Spread half the batter into bottom of baking pan. The dough is sticky and needs to be patted and pushed along to cover bottom of the pan. Hint: use the back of a large metal spoon for easier handling.

Spread apricot filling over the dough.

Add the other half of batter over filling, again carefully patting and pushing the batter to cover filling. This part is tricky. Use a spoon in each hand to spread the dough over the filling. Combine the topping ingredients; sprinkle topping over all.

Bake 30 to 35 minutes or until top is golden brown. Cool 10 minutes before cutting.

MAKES 24 SQUARES

NEW WORLD APRICOT SQUARES

Preserves will work for this version

3½ cups buttermilk baking mix
¼ cup sugar
2 eggs
1½ cups milk
1 jar (12 ounces) apricot preserves

TOPPING

1 cup walnuts
¼ cup sugar

Preheat oven to 350 degrees and lightly grease a 9 × 13-inch baking pan. Combine baking mix, sugar, eggs, and milk; beat by hand 30 seconds. Spread half of the batter into the bottom of the baking pan; spread preserves over the batter. Cover preserves with the other half of the batter. Mix together topping ingredients; sprinkle topping over all.

Bake 30 to 35 minutes or until top is golden brown. Cool 10 minutes before cutting.

MAKES 24 SQUARES

FRESH APPLE-NUT CAKE
Almás-Diós Sütemény

This is an easy-to-make moist cake. Rich and flavorful, this single-layer cake needs no frosting.

Grease and flour a 9 × 13-inch baking pan.

3 eggs
1¾ cups sugar
2 cups flour
1 teaspoon baking soda
1 teaspoon cinnamon
½ teaspoon salt
1 cup vegetable oil
1 teaspoon vanilla
4 cups apples, peeled and sliced thin (any variety)
1 cup chopped walnuts

Preheat oven to 350 degrees.

Beat eggs and sugar until thick.

Sift flour, baking soda, cinnamon, and salt. Stir into egg mixture. Add oil and vanilla; mix well. Stir in apples and walnuts.

Pour in cake pan and bake 50 to 60 minutes. Cake will pull away from the sides of the pan when done.

MAKES 24 SQUARES

Dilled Cream Cheese Cake.

DILLED CREAM CHEESE CAKE
Kapros Túrós Lepény

Thank goodness my mother had recorded this recipe just as she had made it through the years. I would not have been able to create this family favorite according to the directions in her much used cookbook, *Hungarian Cookery*, published in 1931.

> *"Mix 1 pound of flour and ½ pound butter, or 2 spoonsful of lard. Stir in 3 whole eggs, 3 tablespoonsful of sour cream, ¾ ounce of yeast, soaked in milk, and sufficient amount of milk to have a good firm dough. Knead well and let it rise. Meanwhile squeeze 1 plateful of pot cheese through a sieve, stir in 10 whole eggs, 1 quart of sour cream, a pinch of salt, 6 tablespoonsful of flour and finely chopped dill; mix thoroughly. Roll out dough ½ inch in thickness, put in pan and spread with the above mixture. Brush top with beaten eggs and bake in a slow oven. When done, cut in squares and serve."*

CRUST

- ½ pound cold margarine
- 2 cups flour
- 3 egg yolks (reserve whites for filling)
- ½ envelope powdered yeast
- ⅓ cup warm milk
- ½ cup sugar

Cream Cheese Filling

1 cup sugar

4 packages (3 ounces each) cream cheese, at room temperature

4 egg yolks

16 ounces cottage cheese

½ teaspoon dried dill or 2 teaspoons finely chopped fresh dill

1 teaspoon vanilla

4 egg whites plus 3 reserved whites

Preheat oven to 350 degrees.

Cut margarine into flour until mixture forms small balls the size of peas. Add yolks. Dissolve yeast in the warm milk and add to flour mixture. Blend in sugar and mix until all ingredients are blended.

Pat dough into a 9 × 13-inch baking pan; go 2 inches up the sides. Dough will be sticky. Hint: Use the back of a large metal spoon to spread dough evenly over the bottom of the pan.

Beat sugar into cream cheese until smooth. Add egg yolks, cottage cheese, dill, and vanilla. Mix thoroughly. Beat egg whites until stiff and fold into cheese mixture.

Pour filling into prepared crust. Mother baked this in her gas oven at 350 degrees 45 to 60 minutes. In my electric oven the cake bakes at 325 degrees for about 50 minutes. If edges brown too rapidly, reduce temperature by 25 degrees. When done, the filling should be lightly brown and the center firm.

Cool completely before cutting into serving pieces.

Makes 24 squares

JAM AND MERINGUE CAKE
Linzer Szelet

An Austrian delicacy, this dessert found its way into Hungarian kitchens many years ago. There are numerous variations of linzer cake; some include a complicated lattice-patterned top woven with strips of dough. I prefer this simplified version.

3 cups flour
⅔ cup sugar
2½ teaspoons baking powder
¼ pound margarine
½ cup sour cream
3 egg yolks
½ teaspoon vanilla
2 cups apricot or prune filling (see page 173)

MERINGUE
3 egg whites
6 tablespoons sugar
¾ cup ground walnuts

Preheat oven to 350 degrees.

Sift the flour, sugar, and baking powder into a large bowl. Cut in margarine, until it resembles oatmeal. Add sour cream, egg yolks, and vanilla. Mix well.

Pat into a 9 × 13-inch baking pan (dough will be sticky). Spread apricot filling over top. Bake for 35 to 45 minutes or until crust is light brown.

While cake is baking, whip together egg whites and sugar to a stiff consistency. Spread meringue on top of baked cake and sprinkle with nuts. Return to oven and bake until meringue is light brown, 5 to 7 minutes.

Allow to cool and cut into squares.

MAKES 20 TO 24 SQUARES

HUNGARIAN CREPE SUZETTES
Palacsinta

We see the French influence in these thin pancakes that can take any kind of filling. Hungarians like to eat them as a dessert, favoring a sweetened cottage cheese filling. Dry or farmer's cheese is best for this, but if your store doesn't carry dry cottage cheese, use regular small curd cottage cheese. Crepes taste best when served warm. To reheat, place in a buttered baking dish, cover with foil and heat in an oven warmed to 325 degrees for 20 minutes.

Batter

1 egg, slightly beaten
1 cup milk
½ teaspoon vanilla extract
1 cup flour
1½ teaspoons sugar
Pinch salt
Butter for pan

Filling

1 package (8 ounces) cream cheese, at room temperature
½ cup sugar
1 egg yolk
1 teaspoon vanilla
16 ounces dry cottage cheese

Garnish

3 tablespoons sour cream, at room temperature
1 teaspoon sugar
Strawberry or cherry preserves, optional

Combine egg, milk, and vanilla in one bowl; mix flour, sugar, and salt in another bowl.

Add wet ingredients to the dry; beat with electric mixer until smooth. Batter will be thin.

Butter a 10-inch skillet and heat until a drop of water sizzles in the butter. Pour in ¼ cup batter tilting skillet until the batter spreads evenly over the bottom. When the edge of pancake starts to look dry, turn it over with a spatula and lightly brown other side. Remove to a warm dish and continue until all the batter has been cooked. Always butter the skillet after each pancake.

For the filling, beat together cream cheese and sugar; mix in egg yolk and vanilla. Stir cottage cheese into the mixture until well blended.

Place 2 tablespoons filling near the edge of each pancake and roll into a cylinder shape. Place into ovenproof dish with seam of the pancake on the bottom.

For the garnish, mix sour cream and sugar until sugar dissolves. Spoon over rolled crepes. Strawberry or cherry preserves make a colorful garnish,

MAKES 12 CREPES

Baked Crescent Cookies

NUT-FILLED CRESCENT COOKIES
Dios Kifli

I offer two versions. Each is equally delicious. The first recipe calls for sour cream and eggs and has a light, flaky texture when baked, while the second version is made with cream cheese, without eggs, and delivers more of a sweet, biscuit-like taste and feel.

Other fillings for these cookies are apricot butter and prune butter (*lekvár*). This is a thick puree made of dried apricots or prunes. Jam or preserves will not work; they will ooze out of your cookies during baking. You can make these fillings yourself, (see recipe below) or you can buy them in 12-ounce jars at the local European market.

Mom's Version

½ pound butter
½ pound margarine
4 cups flour
4 egg yolks (reserve 1 egg white for filling)
1 carton (16 ounces) sour cream
Powdered sugar

Walnut Filling

2 cups ground walnuts
½ cup sugar
1 egg white, slightly beaten
1 teaspoon vanilla
1 teaspoon grated lemon zest

Cut butter and margarine into flour as you would for pie, until shortening and flour cling together. In a medium bowl, blend yolks with sour cream and add to flour mixture. Mix well and divide into 4 sections. Roll each section into a ball (dough will be sticky), wrap each ball in its own plastic wrap and refrigerate for several hours or overnight.

Preheat oven to 350 degrees.

Mix together all the walnut filling ingredients.

Flour a pastry board and rolling pin with plenty of flour or powdered sugar. Roll out one ball of dough at a time (leave the others in the refrigerator to wait their turn) to ⅛-inch thickness (this will roll out to make a 12 × 14-inch rectangle). If dough sticks to board, dust top and bottom of dough with more flour or powdered sugar until dough rolls out smoothly.

Cut dough into 3-inch squares using a knife or a serrated cutting wheel. Place about 2 teaspoons (you don't need to measure, just "eyeball" it) filling near one corner of a square and roll diagonally from that corner to the opposite corner. Place the seam on the bottom, and shape the cookie into a crescent (think "new moon").

Continue until all four balls of dough have been rolled out, cut into squares, filled and shaped into crescents. Place cookies on an un-greased cookie sheet, 1 inch apart, on the middle rack of your oven. Bake until the tops are golden, about 35 to 45 minutes. Check the cookies after 35 minutes. (In my electric oven I bake the cookies at 325 degrees for 35 minutes).

Allow cookies to cool 5 minutes. Remove from cookie sheet. When completely cooled, sprinkle with powdered sugar. Cookies can be stored in an airtight container up to a week.

MAKES 5 TO 6 DOZEN COOKIES

GRANDMA KISH'S CRESCENTS

Each filling recipe makes enough to fill 40 cookies.

¼ pound butter, at room temperature
¼ pound margarine, at room temperature
1 package (8 ounces) cream cheese
¼ cup sugar
1 teaspoon vanilla
2 cups flour
½ teaspoon baking powder
Powdered sugar

Walnut Filling

½ cup milk
½ cup sugar
2 cups ground walnuts
1 tablespoon butter

Apricot or Prune Filling

8 ounces dried apricots or prunes (pitted)
½ cup water
¾ cup sugar

Mix butter, margarine, cream cheese, sugar, and vanilla. Beat by hand or electric mixer until light and fluffy.

Sift flour and baking powder. Add to butter mixture and blend well. Add more flour if dough is sticky.

Pinch out a piece of dough about the size of a walnut and roll into a ball. Proceed with remainder of dough until you have about 40 balls in all. Place on a large plate, cover and refrigerate overnight.

Preheat oven to 350 degrees.

Make the filling of your choice. For the walnut filling, heat milk; add sugar and walnuts. Stir in butter. Cook on low heat only until butter is dissolved. Cool slightly before spooning on rounds of dough.

For apricot or prune filling, place fruit in a saucepan; add sugar and ½ cup water (just enough to cover fruit). Bring to a boil, then lower heat and simmer, uncovered, until fruit is soft and liquid has been absorbed. Stir occasionally. Do not allow water to evaporate and fruit to burn. Add more water if needed until fruit becomes soft (about 8 minutes). Cool; puree in blender or food processor. Any leftover filling can be stored in the refrigerator in a covered container for up to a year.

Flour your board and rolling pin and roll each ball of dough into a circle about ⅛ inch thick. Place 1 rounded teaspoon filling on the edge of circle of dough. Roll up and gently push into a crescent shape, placing rolled edge on the bottom.

Bake on an ungreased cookie sheet for about 20 minutes or until light brown. When cool, sprinkle with powdered sugar.

MAKES 40 COOKIES

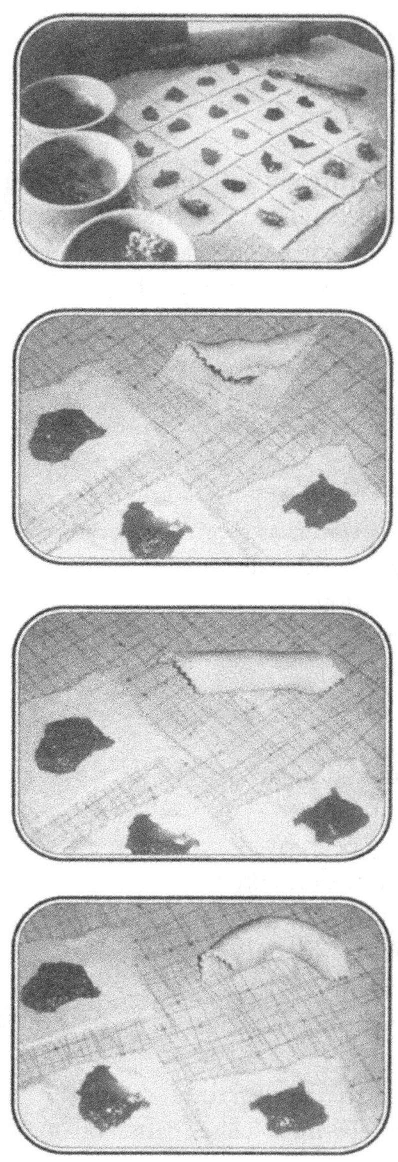

Making Crescent Cookies.

WALNUT TORTE
Dios Torta

The French introduced mouth-watering tortes to the Hungarians at the beginning of the nineteenth century. These rich cakes are made with a large amount of eggs, a fair amount of walnuts, and a little flour. Butter frosting adds to the moistness of this two-layer cake, our family's favorite for celebrating birthdays (or any other days).

12 eggs, yolks separated from whites
1 cup sugar
Pinch of salt
2 tablespoons water, at room temperature
1 cup finely ground walnuts
5 tablespoons flour
1 teaspoon vanilla

BUTTER FROSTING

½ cup milk
¾ cup granulated sugar
3 tablespoons flour
1 egg, slightly beaten
1 tablespoon instant coffee
½ pound butter
3 tablespoons powdered sugar
1 teaspoon vanilla
½ cup finely ground walnuts

Preheat oven to 350 degrees.

Prepare two 10-inch cake pans: oil-spray bottoms; press wax paper cut to fit into the bottom of each pan, then turn oiled side of paper up to receive batter. (Note: This recipe may be baked in a 9 × 13-inch baking pan prepared in the same way as for round pans).

Beat together egg yolks, sugar, and salt until thick, about 10 minutes. Add water and beat another 2 minutes.

Add walnuts, flour, and vanilla; mix well.

Beat egg whites until stiff and fold into the egg yolk mixture gently so as not to break down the whipped egg whites.

Pour into prepared pans and bake about 20 minutes. Use a toothpick to check for doneness.

Cool completely before removing from pans to frost.

To make the frosting, in a medium saucepan, combine milk, granulated sugar, flour, egg, and coffee. Stirring constantly, cook until thick enough to coat a wooden spoon, about 7 minutes. Cool 10 minutes.

Add butter, powdered sugar and vanilla. Beat with an electric mixer for 10 minutes. The frosting will thicken upon beating.

Frost top of the bottom layer and place top layer over the bottom. Frost top and sides of cake. Sprinkle walnuts evenly over the top. Refrigerate until an hour before serving.

SERVES 12

Slice of Walnut Torte with Butter Frosting.

WALNUT ROLL
Dios Kalács

This classic dessert is usually reserved for special occasions and holidays. Preparation is not as complicated as it may seem at first glance. The secret is to dissolve the yeast in milk that has been warmed to the correct temperature (110 degrees). Rather than relying on guesswork, use a thermometer. If liquid is too hot, or not warm enough, dough will not rise.

Nut Filling

1 pound plus ½ cup walnuts, ground medium
½ cup sugar
2 egg whites, slightly beaten (reserve yolks)

Dough

2 packages dry yeast or 2 yeast cakes
½ cup warm milk
6 cups flour
½ teaspoon salt
½ cup sugar
½ pound unsalted butter, melted
1 cup sour cream
3 eggs, beaten

To make filling, blend nuts, sugar, and egg whites and set aside.

To make the dough, dissolve yeast in warm milk (allow 5 minutes). Sift together flour, salt, and sugar in a large bowl; set aside. Combine milk/yeast mixture, butter, sour cream, and eggs in another large bowl. Add dry mixture and stir until well blended. Place dough on a floured board and knead until dough is smooth and elastic (about 10 minutes). If you have an electric mixer, let the dough hook accessory do the work for you.

Divide dough into 4 equal parts. With a rolling pin, roll one section at a time into a 10 × 14-inch rectangle. Spread each section with the nut filling. Roll up the dough and filling (long side) and place on two greased cookie sheets (two rolls to each cookie sheet).

Let rise in a draft-free room at a temperature of 85 degrees until double in size. To provide the desirable temperature, preheat oven for 1 minute until just warmed, then turn off. Place cookie sheets in oven. Rising time will take about 1 to 1½ hours.

While dough is rising, prepare egg wash. Mix 2 reserved egg yolks with 1 tablespoon water. Brush on nut rolls just before baking.

Preheat oven to 350 degrees.

Bake one cookie sheet at a time (unless you have a super-wide oven) 30 to 40 minutes, or until rolls are golden brown. Allow dough to cool before slicing.

MAKES FOUR 14-INCH ROLLS

Variations:

Poppy seed filling may be used instead of walnuts.

POPPY SEED FILLING

1 pound ground poppy seed
¾ cup sugar
½ cup hot milk
1 teaspoon lemon rind
1 teaspoon lemon juice
1 cup white raisins, optional

Combine all the ingredients and mix well. Cool filling before spreading on dough.

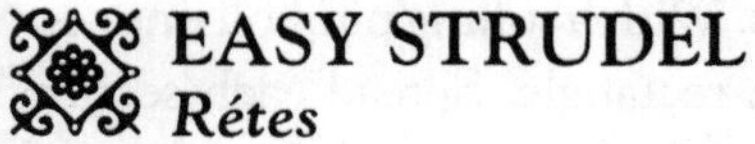

EASY STRUDEL
Rétes

This exquisite pastry requires not only time, but a great deal of experience to make. To achieve the desired flakiness, the dough must be stretched paper thin. One must know just how far this dough can be stretched without tearing it. To watch an experienced chef or cook gently pull at the sheet of dough with the back of her hand is to watch an artist at work.

Today, modern cooks have the convenience of filo dough, an uncooked pastry that has already been pulled to a fine thinness. This product is found in the freezer section with the desserts.

Even a novice can make strudel in a fraction of the time it took our grandmothers to produce this flaky dessert. Choose any of the fillings presented here and, voila, you have created the "queen" of pastries.

1 pound filo dough
¼ pound butter or margarine, melted

Preheat oven to 350 degrees.

When all the ingredients (including the filling) are assembled, unwrap and unfold the sheets of filo dough. Cover them with a damp towel to prevent drying when not in use. Trim to fit a 9 × 13-inch baking pan. Butter bottom of pan well. Layer 4 sheets (one atop the other) of filo pastry; brush each sheet with melted butter.

Spread the filling of your choice over pastry. Top with 4 more sheets of filo, brushing each sheet with butter. Spread another layer of filling; top with 4 more filo sheets, brushing each sheet with butter. Spread the last layer of filling over filo, cover with remaining filo, brushing each sheet with remaining butter. Brush top layer with butter.

Bake 1 hour or until the top is golden. Let stand 10 minutes before cutting into squares. Serve warm.

SERVES 10 TO12

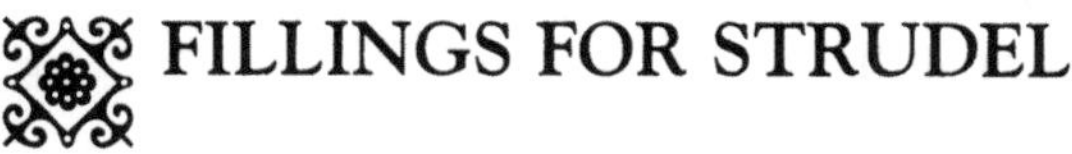

FILLINGS FOR STRUDEL

POPPY SEED FILLING

½ pound ground poppy seeds
1 cup hot milk
¾ cup sugar
¼ cup golden raisins, optional
Juice and zest of ½ lemon

Mix all ingredients well and spread over dough as directed above.

APPLE FILLING

6 large baking apples (Pippin or Granny smith), peeled and sliced thin
½ cup golden or dark raisins, optional
½ cup sugar
Juice of ½ lemon
1 teaspoon cinnamon
½ cup fine bread crumbs

Toss apple slices with raisins and sugar. Mix in lemon juice, cinnamon, and bread crumbs. Spread over layers of dough as directed in strudel recipe.

Cottage Cheese Filling

3 egg yolks
1¼ cups sugar
1 pound dry cottage cheese (sold at specialty or European markets)
Grated zest of 1 lemon
½ teaspoon vanilla
3 egg whites, beaten stiff

Beat yolks and sugar. Add cottage cheese gradually, beating smooth after each addition. Add zest and vanilla; fold in egg whites. Spread on layers of dough as directed above.

Cabbage Filling

1 tablespoon salt
1 head cabbage, chopped (use food processor for this)
3 tablespoons vegetable oil
1 tablespoon sugar
½ teaspoon black pepper

Add salt to cabbage and let stand, covered, for 1 hour. Squeeze cabbage to extract most of the liquid. Heat oil; add cabbage, sugar, and pepper; mix and cook, uncovered, until light brown, stirring frequently. Cool slightly and spread on dough as directed in strudel recipe.

BREADS

Acorns were good 'til bread was found.
— Francis Bacon

The ancient Egyptians discovered the secret of yeast, but the history of bread making dates back to the Stone Age. Pre-historic man made solid cakes of bread from stone-crushed barley, wheat, and water. Some historians believe that civilization began when our earliest ancestors realized bread could keep through the winter months to fend off starvation.

Before you embark on the adventure of bread making, allow me to offer a pinch of philosophy. You may regard bread making as time-consuming, and it is. But I ask you to view it as an art, or as a way to stop, take a deep breath, and slow down a bit.

I like to bake when I have the house to myself. Even before I begin gathering my ingredients, I pick out my favorite Hungarian or classical music, turn on the CD player, and I'm ready to create. Yes, you do have to wait for dough to rise, sometimes twice, but there are other things you can do while during the rising time, and the end product is worth the wait.

When you can't be alone, enlist the help of those around. If they are children, show them how to measure accurately, and how to read a thermometer. Teach them the art of kneading dough. If they have ever worked with clay, this will not be foreign to them. Above all, relax and have fun.

KNEADING

Lightly flour a smooth surface. It could be a large breadboard, or a clean counter top. Flour the board and your hands because the dough will be slightly sticky. Work the dough with the heel of both hands, pushing it against the board and away from you. Fold the dough over on itself each time you push and keep turning the dough. Continue kneading the dough for about 10 minutes or until it becomes smooth and elastic. Test for elasticity by gently pulling and stretching a small piece of dough until it forms a thin sheet. The stretched piece should hold together without tearing.

If an electric mixer is used for kneading, place the dough into a large bowl, attach the dough hook and set the speed on low. (A word of caution: the mixer must be heavy-duty with 400 watts of power). Mix for about 10 minutes, or until the dough no longer sticks to the sides of the bowl. Do not over-mix as this will break down the gluten.

ABOUT YEAST

Most American home bakers choose granulated yeast over cake yeast since no refrigeration is needed with the granulated. It is important to dissolve yeast in water at the proper temperature (105-115 degrees). To remove any guesswork, use a roast thermometer that includes a yeast temperature reading. To ensure yeast freshness, check the expiration date on the package. Bread will not rise with stale yeast.

Some recipes call for proofing (foaming) the yeast. To proof, add 1 teaspoon sugar to the yeast that has been dissolved in the amount of water indicated in the recipe, and let it stand for 10 minutes. When the mixture doubles in volume, the yeast is active, or proofed.

RISING

Put the kneaded dough in a lightly oiled ceramic, glass, or stainless steel bowl and cover the bowl with a clean, damp cloth. This will keep the dough from drying out during rising. The room should be draft-free, and at a temperature between 75 to 85 degrees. If the room is cooler than this, put the bowl in a pilot-lit gas oven, or, preheat an electric oven at the lowest temperature for 1 minute. Another alternative to providing the correct temperature is to fill a large pot with hot, steaming water. Place a rack over the pot and put the bowl of dough (covered) on the rack.

The dough should almost double in volume on the first rising. This takes 1 to 2 hours. To determine when the dough has raised enough, press a fingertip into the dough. If the impression remains, the dough is ready to be baked.

TIPS FOR SUCCESS IN BAKING YEAST BREADS

1. Always bring ingredients to room temperature before mixing.

2. Measure accurately.

3. When a recipe calls for "cutting in" the butter or fat, butter must be cold, but lard or shortening can be at room temperature.

4. Oven and liquid temperatures are in Fahrenheit degrees.

5. Unless otherwise indicated, use white, all-purpose flour.

6. Be sure the rising bowl is large enough to accommodate the dough once it has doubled in size.

7. Set convection ovens 50 degrees lower than conventional ovens.

8. Breads bake faster in glass baking pans than in metal ones.

9. To test for doneness: When the loaf has shrunken away from the sides of the baking pan, the bread is usually done. If in doubt, insert a thermometer into the center of the loaf. A baked loaf will register above 190 degrees. With practice, you'll be able to tell just by the appearance and often by the tantalizing aroma that your bread is done.

10. Cool freshly baked bread for one hour before slicing.

ABOUT QUICK BREADS

Quick breads are popular with cooks who want quick results. These recipes do not call for yeast. The leavening agents are baking powder and baking soda. Some recipes require both, some only the powder or the soda.

These breads are more forgiving than yeast breads and offer latitude for substitutions. For example, if the recipe calls for all-purpose flour, whole-wheat flour can be substituted for up to one-third of the all-purpose flour. Granulated and brown sugars are interchangeable, as are butter and oil. Chocolate bits, chopped nuts, raisins, or dried fruit can be added or subtracted in sweet breads. Shredded cheeses, diced chilies, ham or bacon can be added to other quick breads.

Quick breads are usually baked in loaf pans or muffin tins. They are done when a toothpick inserted in the center comes out clean. These breads can be wrapped in plastic and frozen for up to one month.

How can a nation be great if its bread tastes like Kleenex?

— Julia Child

BASIC WHITE BREAD
Fehér Alapkenyér

This is a dense bread that is best sliced thick for toast or sandwiches. It is similar to the homemade bread of my childhood. My sisters and I could hardly wait for the bread to come out of the oven. Our special treat was to sprinkle sugar over the slices. To us, it was the ultimate dessert.

2 cups whole milk
½ cup unsalted butter
1 teaspoon salt
2 tablespoons sugar
2 packages (½ ounce total) active dry yeast
⅔ cup warm water (110-115 degrees)
1 egg, beaten
7 cups all-purpose flour
1 egg, beaten (for egg wash)

In a small saucepan, heat the milk until just below boiling; remove from stove. Add butter, salt, and sugar; stir until melted. Let cool until lukewarm.

In a small bowl, dissolve yeast in warm water. Let stand about 10 minutes, until yeast is completely dissolved.

In a large bowl, combine milk mixture with the yeast mixture. Mix in 1 egg and 3 cups flour. Stir in the remaining flour, 1 cup at a time, beating well after each addition. (If using an electric mixer, be sure it is 400 watts, otherwise you will burn out your motor).

When the dough holds together, turn it out on a lightly floured surface and knead until smooth and elastic, about 10 minutes.

Lightly oil a large bowl, place the dough in the bowl and turn to coat all sides with oil. Cover with a damp cloth and let rise in a warm place until doubled in volume, about 1 hour. (See page 185)

Punch down or deflate the dough and turn it out on a lightly floured surface. Divide the dough into two equal pieces and form into loaves. Place the dough into two lightly greased 9 × 5-inch loaf pans. Cover the loaves with a damp cloth and let rise until dough reaches the tops of the pans, about 20 to 30 minutes.

Preheat oven to 350 degrees.

Brush egg wash over tops of loaves.

Bake 35 to 45 minutes, depending on your oven, or when tops are golden brown. Remove loaves from pans and place on wire racks to cool completely.

YIELD: 2 LOAVES

Basic White Bread.

SOUR CREAM ROLLS
Tejfeles Zsemlye

There's no need to knead this one.

¼ cup warm water (110-115 degrees)
1 package (¼ ounce) active dry yeast
¾ cup sour cream
2 tablespoons sugar
2 tablespoons vegetable oil
1 teaspoon salt
1 large egg
2 cups all-purpose flour

Place water in a large bowl. Sprinkle yeast into the water and stir until dissolved. (See page 185)

Using a long-handled spoon, stir in sour cream, sugar, oil, salt, egg and ¾ cup flour. Beat 2 minutes at medium speed of electric mixer. (Use regular beater blades.)

With hands or a large spoon, mix in remaining flour until well blended and forms a ball. The dough will be sticky.

Cover with a damp cloth; let the dough rise until doubled in volume, about 1½ hours. (See page 185)

Stir down dough. Using a 12-cup, 3-inch greased muffin pan, fill each cup half full.

Cover and let the rolls rise until they are doubled in size, about an hour.

Preheat the oven to 350 degrees.

Bake for 20 to 30 minutes, or until tops are lightly browned.

Remove rolls from pans and cool on a wire rack.

YIELD: 12 ROLLS

LILLIAN'S EASY PEASANT BREAD
Lenke könyü Parasztkenyér

Cousin Lillian shares this recipe for a hearty bread. A family friend brought it from Hungary many years ago. If you like a heavier textured bread with a crunchy crust, this is the recipe for you. It is wonderful with soups and stews.

1 package (¼ ounce) quick-rising yeast
5 cups plus 2 tablespoons all-purpose flour
½ cup warm water (110-115 degrees)
1 tablespoon salt
2 cups boiling water
1 cup warm mashed potatoes

In a small bowl, mix yeast with 2 tablespoons flour and add water. Stir until yeast is dissolved; set aside.

In a large bowl, combine 5 cups flour, salt, and water. Mix until well blended. Add yeast mixture and mashed potatoes.

Leave dough in the bowl and work with fingers until dough forms a ball. Cover with a towel and let rise until double in size (about 2 hours).

Preheat oven to 400 degrees.

Lightly spray a cookie sheet with oil. Flour hands, place dough on cookie sheet and shape into an oblong loaf.

Put bread into the oven, pull temperature down to 350 degrees and bake 40 to 50 minutes, or until internal temperature reads 200 to 210 degrees.

Remove sheet from the oven and cool bread on a rack.

YIELD: 10 TO 12 SLICES

New World Version

If you don't want to make the mashed potatoes from scratch, you can use commercial frozen mashed potatoes. Just follow the microwave directions on the package. Do not exceed a cup, as this will make the bread too heavy.

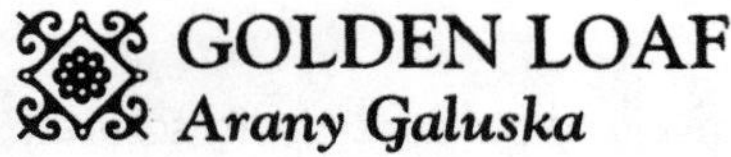

GOLDEN LOAF
Arany Galuska

This is an old Hungarian recipe that is baked in a tube pan.

2 packages (½ ounce total) active dry yeast
1 teaspoon sugar
¾ cup warm water (110-115 degrees)
1 cup hot whole milk
½ cup sugar
½ cup butter, room temperature
1 teaspoon salt
2 eggs, slightly beaten
5 ½ cups all-purpose flour
2 cups sugar
2 tablespoons ground cinnamon
1 cup walnuts, finely ground
½ cup margarine, melted

In a small bowl, dissolve yeast and sugar in warm water; let stand 8 to 10 minutes. In a large bowl, combine milk, ½ cup sugar, ½ cup butter, and salt. When butter is melted, stir in yeast mixture. Add eggs and mix.

Gradually add flour; mix until dough holds together. Turn out onto a floured surface and knead 10 minutes. Cover; let rise until double, about 1 hour.

Stir down dough; let rest 10 minutes.

In a medium bowl, combine 2 cups sugar, cinnamon and walnuts.

Divide dough into 12 balls, about the size of lemons; using a slotted spoon, dip each ball in melted margarine, then roll in sugar/cinnamon/walnut mixture.

Arrange in a greased 10-inch tube or 12-cup fluted tube pan. (You will have 2 layers). Cover; let rise until double, 1½ to 2 hours. (Any leftover margarine can be drizzled over top of loaf just before baking).

Heat oven to 350 degrees. Bake about 40 minutes or until golden brown. Invert pan onto serving plate.

YIELD: 12 SERVINGS

NEW WORLD VERSION

1 cup granulated sugar
1 cup brown sugar
4 teaspoons ground cinnamon
½ cup chopped nuts (optional)
1 package frozen rolls (24 total), thawed
½ cup butter or margarine, melted

Combine sugars, cinnamon, and nuts. Separate rolls and coat each with butter, then with sugar mixture.

Layer the rolls in well-greased 9- or 12-cup tube pan. Let rise in a warm place until double in size, 1½ to 2 hours.

Preheat oven to 350 degrees. Bake for 35 to 40 minutes. Cool for 1 or 2 minutes, then loosen edges and turn out onto a plate.

YIELD: 12 SERVINGS

HUNGARIAN BRAIDED BREAD
Magyar Fonottkenyér

Sometimes called a wedding bread because it symbolizes the intertwining of two lives, this bread is as pleasing to the eye as well as to the palate.

1 package (¼ ounce) active dry yeast
1¾ cups warm whole milk (110-115 degrees)
3 eggs
2 tablespoons granulated sugar
2 teaspoons salt
5½ cups all-purpose flour
1 tablespoon sesame or poppy seeds
1 egg, beaten

In a small bowl, dissolve yeast in warm milk. Let stand 15 minutes.

In a large bowl, mix together 3 eggs, sugar, and salt.

Add the yeast mixture and 3 cups flour; mix until well blended.

Add the remaining 2½ cups flour, ½ cup at a time, mixing well after each addition. Use your hands when the dough gets too stiff to work with a spoon.

When the dough forms a ball, turn it out onto a floured surface and knead until smooth and elastic, about 8 minutes.

Cut the dough into 3 equal parts and form 3 thin loaves, 20 inches long. Move the 3 loaves to a lightly greased cookie sheet; let the dough rest for 20 minutes.

Pinch the 3 strands of dough together at the top end and braid (just like pigtails). At the bottom, pinch together the three strands. You now have 1 loaf; tuck top and bottom ends under the loaf.

Cover with a towel and let rise until double in size, 40 to 50 minutes.

Preheat oven to 375 degrees.

Brush risen dough with the beaten egg and sprinkle with poppy or sesame seeds.

Bake at 375 degrees for 10 minutes. Reduce heat to 350 degrees and bake for an additional 20 to 40 minutes, or, until golden brown. (In my electric oven, total baking time was 30 minutes).

Cool on cookie sheet for 5 minutes; remove and cool completely on a rack.

YIELD: 1 LOAF

Hungarian Braided Bread.

HUNGARIAN FRIED BREAD
Lángos

This historic recipe, called the ancestor of the popular pizza, was introduced by the Turks during their occupation of Hungary. Hungarians like to eat it topped with sour cream and fresh dill. It is also delicious spread with minced onions and garlic.

1 teaspoon sugar
1 package (¼ ounce) active dry yeast
½ cup lukewarm whole milk
1½ cup all-purpose flour
1 tablespoon vegetable oil
½ cup warm mashed baking potatoes
½ teaspoon salt
1 cup oil, to fry

Mix sugar and yeast into warm milk (110-115 degrees) and let stand for 10 minutes.

Place flour into a large bowl. Make a well in the center and pour in milk/yeast/sugar mixture.

Add oil, warm mashed potatoes, and salt.

Mix together with hands until dough holds together. Put dough on a smooth surface and knead for about 15 minutes, adding a little flour to the kneading board if it becomes sticky.

Cover with a damp cloth and let rise for about an hour, or, until the dough has doubled in size.

After dough has risen, flour hands and divide into 4 pieces; shape each into round, flat cake about the size of a dessert plate. The cakes will puff up during frying.

Heat oil to medium-high in a 10-inch skillet and fry cakes (do not cover) 3 to 5 minutes on each side. They should be light brown on both sides.

Drain on paper towels. Salt lightly and spread with your favorite topping. (Try it with powdered sugar sprinkled over the top). *Lángos* tastes best when eaten hot.

YIELD: 4 SERVINGS

NEW WORLD VERSION

Preheat oven to 375 degrees.

Follow the above recipe. Instead of frying, place the cakes on a lightly greased cookie sheet and bake for about 15 minutes, or until golden.

BEER BREAD STICKS
Sörkenykenyér Pálca

The children will enjoy helping to roll the dough into sticks—like playing with clay.

1 package (¼ ounce) active dry yeast
¾ cup warm water
¾ cup vegetable oil
¾ cup beer, at room temperature
4 cups all-purpose flour
Garlic salt
3 tablespoons butter, melted

In a large bowl, dissolve yeast in warm water. Stir in oil and beer. Gradually stir in flour and mix until flour is well incorporated. Cover; let rise in a warm place until double (1½ hours to 2 hours).

Heat oven to 350 degrees. Grease 2 cookie sheets; sprinkle sheets with garlic salt.

Stir down dough. Pull out walnut-sized pieces of dough. Shape each piece into sticks 8-inches long. Sticks should be thin, no bigger than the width of two pencils. Hint: A 12 × 12-inch plastic cutting board is ideal for shaping the dough into sticks. Just roll them out with your hands.

Place on prepared cookie sheets. Brush sticks with melted butter and sprinkle tops with garlic salt. Bake 20 to 30 minutes, until golden in color.

YIELD: 3 TO 4 DOZEN

BEER PRETZELS
Sörperec

Use the Beer Bread Sticks recipe, facing. Shape the dough into sticks. Take each end of the stick and loop them toward the center, crisscrossing one end over the other until you have the shape of a bow or a pretzel. Brush tops with melted butter and sprinkle coarse salt over all.

PECAN SPIRALS
Csavart Diós Kenyér

2 cups all-purpose flour
2 tablespoons granulated sugar
1 tablespoon baking powder
½ teaspoon salt
½ cup cold butter
1 egg
½ cup whole milk, room temperature
1 tablespoon butter, melted
¼ cup finely chopped pecans
3 tablespoons brown sugar

Preheat oven to 400 degrees.

Combine flour, sugar, baking powder, and salt; mix well.

Cut butter into flour mixture until mixture resembles coarse crumbs. Combine the egg and milk, and add to flour mixture. Stir until dough clings together.

Place dough on a floured board. Knead 12 to 15 times. Roll dough into an 8 by 15-inch rectangle. Brush melted butter on the dough.

Combine pecans and brown sugar; sprinkle over dough. Gently press the mixture into the dough. Fold dough in half, lengthwise.

Cut dough into 1-inch strips—you'll have 15 strips. Twist each strip into a spiral; pinch together the cut ends of each strip to keep the spiral from unwinding. Place on a lightly greased cookie sheet.

Bake about 10 minutes until lightly browned.

YIELD: 15 SPIRALS

CRANBERRY WALNUT BREAD
Áfonya és Dióskenyér

½ cup butter
1 cup sugar
2 eggs
1 teaspoon vanilla extract
2 cups all-purpose flour
1 teaspoon baking soda
½ teaspoon ground cinnamon
½ teaspoon salt
⅓ cup orange juice
¾ cup canned whole-berry cranberry sauce
½ cup coarsely chopped walnuts

Preheat oven to 350 degrees.

Grease and flour an 8 × 4-inch loaf pan.

In a large bowl, using an electric mixer, cream butter and sugar until smooth. Beat in eggs and vanilla.

In a separate bowl, combine flour, baking soda, cinnamon, and salt; mix well. Add this dry combination to egg mixture, alternating with orange juice. Mix by hand just until blended to avoid over-mixing.

Fold in cranberry sauce and walnuts. Turn into loaf pan. The dough will be thick; use the back of a spoon to smooth out the surface.

Bake 50 to 60 minutes or until wood pick inserted into the center comes out clean.

Cool in pan 10 minutes. Remove from pan and cool completely on wire rack.

YIELD: 1 LOAF

New World Version

Prepare 1 package (15.6 ounces) Cranberry Quick Bread Mix according to package directions, substituting orange juice for water. Fold in cranberry sauce and walnuts and bake as directed above.

CARROT WALNUT BREAD
Sárgarépa és Dióskenyér

This recipe only requires one bowl in its preparation, making it quick to prepare and easy to clean up afterwards.

2 cups all-purpose flour
1 cup chopped walnuts
½ cup granulated sugar
½ cup packed brown sugar
2 teaspoons baking powder
1 teaspoon ground cinnamon
½ teaspoon salt
3 medium carrots, finely shredded (about 3 cups)
½ cup whole milk
⅓ cup vegetable oil
1 egg

Preheat oven to 350 degrees. Grease and flour one 9 × 5-inch loaf pan.

In a large bowl, combine flour, nuts, sugars, baking powder, cinnamon, and salt and stir until well blended.

Add carrots, milk, oil, and egg; mix until just moistened.

Spoon the dough into loaf pan and smooth out surface. Bake 45 to 55 minutes, or, until it passes the toothpick test.

Cool in the pan for 10 minutes, then turn out onto a rack. When completely cool, wrap in foil until ready to eat. If desired, the loaf may be kept in the freezer up to 1 month.

YIELD: 10 TO 12 SLICES

ZUCCHINI ALMOND LOAF
Tök és Mandulacipó

This recipe makes two loaves and keeps well when wrapped properly for storage.

3 eggs
1 cup sugar
1 cup vegetable oil
1 tablespoon vanilla extract
3 cups all-purpose flour
1 teaspoon salt
2 teaspoons ground cinnamon
1 teaspoon baking soda
¼ teaspoon baking powder
2 cups grated zucchini (3 medium zucchini)
1 cup toasted and chopped almonds
Honey, optional
Slivered almonds, optional

Preheat oven to 350 degrees; grease two 9 × 5-inch loaf pans.

In a large bowl, beat eggs with an electric beater. Add sugar, oil, and vanilla until well blended with eggs. Stir in zucchini.

In a separate bowl, combine flour, salt, cinnamon, baking soda, and baking powder; add to zucchini mixture. Mix well; stir in almonds.

Spoon into two loaf pans and bake 40 to 50 minutes. Loaves are done when toothpick inserted into the center comes out clean.

Cool in the pans for 10 minutes; then remove loaves from pans and cool thoroughly. If desired, brush tops of loaves with honey and decorate with almonds.

Wrap in plastic to keep fresh. To freeze, wrap in foil,

YIELD: 24 SLICES

LEMON BREAD
Citrom Kenyér

Lemon Bread is a light, refreshing dessert, especially after a heavy meal.

¾ cup margarine
1¼ cups sugar
3 eggs
2½ cups all-purpose flour
2 teaspoons baking powder
1 teaspoon salt
½ cup whole milk
⅓ cup lemon juice
2 teaspoons grated lemon peel

Preheat oven to 350 degrees. Grease and flour a 9 × 5-inch loaf pan.

Cream margarine and sugar until light and fluffy. Blend in eggs.

Combine flour, baking powder, and salt; add to wet mixture alternately with milk and juice, mixing well after each addition. Stir in peel.

Pour into loaf pan. Bake 60 to 70 minutes, or until a toothpick inserted into the center comes out clean.

Cool 5 minutes, remove from pan and cool completely on a rack.

YIELD: 1 LOAF

Wines

WINES
Magyar Bor

Hungary has always placed a great deal of importance on its wine culture. So much so, that it is the only country with a national anthem that contains a line paying tribute to its wines:

"*On the grapevines of Tokaj, Thou dripped nectar...*"

For 3,000 years Hungary had a tradition of producing fine wine. Then the country came under communist rule, and wine output dropped dramatically. After the fall of communism, Hungary labored hard to re-establish its own style of wine and regain its reputation in the world of winemaking. It is now attracting foreign investors who are anxious to expand the Hungarian wine culture.

Bull's Blood (*Bikavér)*, probably the best known of exported Hungarian wines, is made from several grape varieties grown in a region called Eger. Volcanic soil in the hills surrounding Eger and abundant sunlight makes Eger the ideal place to grow excellent varietal grapes. It is a sharp, full-bodied red wine often served with beef or pork.

One legend behind the name of Bull's Blood goes back to 1552 during a battle between the Hungarian and the Turkish armies. When the Hungarian troops became weary, they stopped at wine cellars to refresh themselves. Going back into battle, the soldiers must have looked fierce with wine running down their beards and clothing. The Turks, who thought of the Hungarians as rabid, blood-thirsty adversaries believed these descendants of Attila the Hun had been drinking the blood of a bull and fled.

Another popular wine, the Blue Oporto (*Kékoporto)*, comes from grapes grown in a warm climate such as that found in Villany and Szekszárd. It is usually blended with *Kékfrankos*. Also known as *Nagyburgundi*, *Kékfrankos* is made from purple grapes and results in a very dry wine when grapes are grown in colder areas like Sopron, near the Austrian border.

A grape that helped popularize Hungary's red wine was the Kardarka grape. It is believed the Serbs brought this grape to the Szekszárd region as early as the sixteenth century. Extremely popular by the nineteenth century, it was almost eliminated under communism. It matures well and is a key constituent of Bull's Blood. An old story tells us that Franz Liszt had acquired quite a fondness for Kardarka wine and often visited the Szekszárd region to imbibe. Legend says he composed the "Szekszárd March" under the influence of this heady wine.

Other red wines that Hungary produces at respectable levels are Cabernet, Merlot, and Pinot Noir.

One of the more popular white wines is Tokaj (pronounced tok-eye), made from the furmint grape. Named for the region in which it grows, Tokaj develops the aroma of honey and walnuts after aging in wood. In the seventeenth century, Tokaj was known as the wine of kings and became a favorite among the royal households of Europe. Today, it is served mostly as a dessert wine.

Tramini is a spicy, reddish grape that produces a golden, yellow wine. Its fragrance suggests a touch of rose and apricot with a Muscat-like aroma and is grown in several regions across Hungary.

The yellow Muscat (*Muskotály*) grape produces a bouquet reminiscent of orange blossoms. When overripe, it produces a dessert wine. This grape grows best in cooler areas like Tokaj.

A purplish-red grape called Pinot gris (*Szürkebarát*) makes a pale gold wine. Though it produces a sweet wine when its sugar content is high, wine connoisseurs enjoy it best in its dry version. This is considered the most famous wine to come from the *Badacsony* region.

Léanyka (little girl or maiden) is an ancient grape cultured for centuries by Hungarian vintners and yields a greenish-white wine. It grows mainly in the *Eger* region and is served as a dessert wine.

Linden Leaf (*Harslevelu)* makes a wine that is greenish-yellow in color with a light, fruity aroma. Wine connoisseurs like to serve this as an accompaniment to game birds such as pheasant and wild duck.

No matter where the grapes are grown, Hungarians vintners celebrate the harvest with music and singing in anticipation of the fine wines that will soon be pouring from the barrels.

INDEX

www.ingramcontent.com/pod-product-compliance
Lightning Source LLC
Jackson TN
JSHW011359130125
77033JS00023B/756

* 9 7 8 0 7 8 1 8 1 2 4 0 5 *